Echoes from the Backwoods

or, Sketches of Transatlantic Life

VOLUME 1

R.G.A. LEVINGE

CAMBRIDGE
UNIVERSITY PRESS

CAMBRIDGE UNIVERSITY PRESS

Cambridge, New York, Melbourne, Madrid, Cape Town,
Singapore, São Paolo, Delhi, Tokyo, Mexico City

Published in the United States of America by Cambridge University Press, New York

www.cambridge.org
Information on this title: www.cambridge.org/9781108033510

This edition first published 1846
This digitally printed version 2011

ISBN 978-1-108-03351-0 Paperback

CAMBRIDGE LIBRARY COLLECTION

Books of enduring scholarly value

Travel and Exploration

The history of travel writing dates back to the Bible, Caesar, the Vikings and the Crusaders, and its many themes include war, trade, science and recreation. Explorers from Columbus to Cook charted lands not previously visited by Western travellers, and were followed by merchants, missionaries, and colonists, who wrote accounts of their experiences. The development of steam power in the nineteenth century provided opportunities for increasing numbers of 'ordinary' people to travel further, more economically, and more safely, and resulted in great enthusiasm for travel writing among the reading public. Works included in this series range from first-hand descriptions of previously unrecorded places, to literary accounts of the strange habits of foreigners, to examples of the burgeoning numbers of guidebooks produced to satisfy the needs of a new kind of traveller - the tourist.

Echoes from the Backwoods

A dynamic army officer and sportsman, Sir Richard Levinge (1811–84) was an unlikely chronicler of nature. However, service during the suppression of the French Canadian uprising of 1837–8 led to a personal fascination with the people, flora and fauna of the Canadian colonies. Published in 1846, this two-volume description of travel through eastern Canada and the United States reflects the author's passion for hunting and the outdoor life. In Volume 1, the reader accompanies Levinge on his voyage to Newfoundland before being regaled with tales of skating, sleighing, hunting for wolves and a fortnight in the bush in Nova Scotia. The American stage of his travels is lightened by anecdotes of 'Yankees shaving' and 'frigid Baptists'. Illustrated with dramatic lithographs of moose and salmon spearing, this work conveys both the dangers and the attractions for the hunter and traveller of the North American continent at this period.

Cambridge University Press has long been a pioneer in the reissuing of out-of-print titles from its own backlist, producing digital reprints of books that are still sought after by scholars and students but could not be reprinted economically using traditional technology. The Cambridge Library Collection extends this activity to a wider range of books which are still of importance to researchers and professionals, either for the source material they contain, or as landmarks in the history of their academic discipline.

Drawing from the world-renowned collections in the Cambridge University Library, and guided by the advice of experts in each subject area, Cambridge University Press is using state-of-the-art scanning machines in its own Printing House to capture the content of each book selected for inclusion. The files are processed to give a consistently clear, crisp image, and the books finished to the high quality standard for which the Press is recognised around the world. The latest print-on-demand technology ensures that the books will remain available indefinitely, and that orders for single or multiple copies can quickly be supplied.

The Cambridge Library Collection will bring back to life books of enduring scholarly value (including out-of-copyright works originally issued by other publishers) across a wide range of disciplines in the humanities and social sciences and in science and technology.

Drawn by Capt.ⁿ Leveuge

THE AIR HOLE.

London, Pub.ᵈ by H.Colburn,13 G.ᵗ Marlborough S.ᵗ

Day & Haghe Lith.ʳˢ to the Queen.

ECHOES

FROM

THE BACKWOODS;

OR

SKETCHES

OF

TRANSATLANTIC LIFE.

BY

CAPTAIN R. G. A. LEVINGE.

IN TWO VOLUMES.

VOL. I.

LONDON:

HENRY COLBURN, PUBLISHER,

GREAT MARLBOROUGH STREET.

1846.

TO

SIR RICHARD SUTTON, BART.,

OF

COTTESMORE,

ONE OF ENGLAND'S BEST SPORTSMEN,

𝕿𝖍𝖊𝖘𝖊 𝖗𝖔𝖚𝖌𝖍 𝕾𝖐𝖊𝖙𝖈𝖍𝖊𝖘

OF

TRANSATLANTIC LIFE

ARE INSCRIBED BY

THE AUTHOR.

PREFACE.

It is much to be regretted, by every one who has at heart the promotion of British prosperity, that the province of New Brunswick should be so little known in England; that a colony containing many millions of acres of excellent land, magnificent rivers, inexhaustible mineral wealth, and most extensive coal-fields, should be passed over as unheeded as if it belonged not to the British empire. Even in Parliament the advantages of emigration to Canada or the United States are frequently expatiated upon in glowing and persuasive terms, but very rarely is any notice taken of New Brunswick.

Owing to the diffusion of information, by
means of numerous publications respecting
our other northern colonies, the stream of
emigration has been directed that way; so
that, though some thousands who have left
their homes in the Old World in search of
new abodes annually find their way to the
shores of this our nearest colony, yet few,
and those of the most indigent class only,
remain.   In Canada, moreover, where public
works have been of late years carried on, the
government and private companies have held
out strong inducement to emigrants by as-
sisting them to procure lands; while the
great public enterprises continually going
on in the United States attract the great
majority of the labouring classes, especially
Irish, who eventually become settlers.

   In none of our colonies does the agricultural settler find so many advantages as in

New Brunswick. In the counties of Gloucester and Restigouche, the most northern
parts of the province, have been grown excellent crops of wheat ; and scarcely an instance can be adduced in which the crop of
grain of any kind has failed ; whilst, in the pro-
duction of potatoes and other nutritious
roots, New Brunswick cannot be excelled.

Lord Sydenham, in a letter to Lord John
Russell, which accompanied his Report on
Emigration to Upper Canada, observes :—
" Give me yeomen, with a few hundred
pounds each, who will buy cleared farms,
not throw themselves into the Bush, and I
will ensure them comforts and independence
at the end of a couple of years—pigs, pork,
flour, potatoes, horses to ride, cows to milk,
but you must eat all you produce, for devil
a purchaser is to be found : however, the
man's wants are supplied and those of his

family; he has no rent or taxes to pay, and he ought to be satisfied."

So said Lord Sydenham of Canada; and all this is true in regard to New Brunswick, with this essential and striking difference, that in New Brunswick there *is* a market, and a man may not only supply his own wants and those of his family, but actually accumulate money from the sale of his surplus produce. And, above all, nowhere are the liberties so dear to Englishmen to be enjoyed in a higher degree than in this province. It is therefore to be hoped that the time is not far distant when a spur shall be given to enterprise; when the tide of emigration, instead of flowing through this magnificent colony, shall be arrested in its course; when mining and manufactures shall give employment to thousands of workmen, who, from the lack of such sources in our own colonies, are forced to seek them in the United States.

In placing before the public these volumes, the author takes leave to premise that, favourable as may appear to be the picture which he draws of New Brunswick, he has no schemes of speculators or adventurers to second, neither is he biassed by any motive of personal interest; in one or other of which too many works of this nature have originated. His main object has been to present facts and information derived chiefly from his own observation, particularly of a kind likely to prove useful to persons intending to settle in the country of which he treats.

Subjects of less important interest have not been omitted; and he flatters himself that the sportsman in his own chimney-corner in Old England will be gratified, at least, if not warmed, by his account of the

opportunities afforded in New Brunswick for
the display of skill and dexterity in exercises
in which it may never be his lot to partici-
pate.

Information concerning the haunts of game
in North America is often not to be obtained
at all, and, if so, often not to be relied on.
It frequently happens, therefore, that, after
hard fagging, and great perseverance, just
as the sportsman is obliged to leave the
country, he then, and not till then, discovers their favourite resorts.   Many hints
collected from the Indians, from personal
experience in the pursuit of deer and other
game, of fish and fishing, and of what is
termed wood-craft, are offered to such sportsmen whom accident, inclination, or duty may
lead to the New World.

If Brother Jonathan should feel rather
sore about the sketches of himself and his

hopeful progeny introduced into these volumes, I can assure him in all sincerity
that, if I have nothing extenuated, still less
have I been prompted by the national anti-
pathy too prevalent on his side of the Atlantic to " set down aught in malice."

To the kindness of Mr. Perley I am indebted for some particulars concerning the
remnants of the two Indian tribes still resi-
dent in New Brunswick, and for much sta-
tistical information: This gentleman is a
descendant of that Isaac Perley who first
explored the St. John : he is the head of all
enterprise in the colony, Government Emigration Agent, and last, but not least, Wun-
jeet Sagamore, or head Chief of the Micmacs.

R. G. A. L.

London, June, 1846.

ILLUSTRATIONS.

VOL. I.

1. The Air Hole - - ᴸ - *Frontispiece.*
2. Moose run down - - - - - 160
3. Salmon-spearing by Torchlight - - - 186

VOL. II.

1. Caraboo showing Fight - - - *Frontispiece.*
2. War-dance, Wisconsin - - - - 190
3. "Treeing" a Bear - - - - - 206

CONTENTS

OF

THE FIRST VOLUME.

PREFACE . . . v

CHAPTER I.

VOYAGE OUT.—The Transport Service—Military Life in Country Quarters — Voyage across the Atlantic—Dense Fogs—Banks of Newfoundland—Forests of the New World—"The Maid of the Mist"—River St. John . 1

CHAPTER II.

NEW BRUNSWICK—HINTS FOR EMIGRANTS.—First settlement of the Province—General description—Government—Boundary question—Rivers—"The Stone Wigwam"—Wooden Bridge—Fish—Waterfowl—The Bore—Mineral Productions — Whales — Cod — Mines — Divining Rod—Measures 12

CHAPTER III.

NEW BRUNSWICK—CONTINUED.—Towns — Labrador dogs—Horse-dealing — Cobbett—Agent for " Morrison's

pills"—A fire—Amusing incident—Climate—Lumber, hard
and soft wood—Below *Nero*—Effects of frost—Skating—
Sleighing — Coasting — Sleigh Club — Corn-bin extraordinary—Perilous situation .   .   . 57

CHAPTER IV.

OF THE MILICETE AND MICMAC INDIANS.—Origin of
the Indians, a Quere—Fossil remains—Mr. Gesner—
Micmacs, or " Salt-water" Indians—Boundary between
them and the Milicete—Render homage to the Iroquois
—Council fire still burns—Their *Totems*—Language—
Papoose—Wigwams — Snow-shoes—Patterns —Old John
and Cockney   94

CHAPTER V.

NEW BRUNSWICK.—OF THE BIRDS AND BEASTS.—
Passenger Pigeons—Wild and Water fowl—Novel way of
gunning—Genus Tetrao—Birch and Spruce Partridge—
Humming-birds—Wax-bird—Soirée of Owls—Lucifees—
Skunk—Wild Cat—Novel mode of catching Wolves—
Musk-rat—Porcupine—Hares—Bears and Chimneys—A
sound sleeper—The Governor gammoned .   . 127

CHAPTER VI.

NEW BRUNSWICK.—OF THE DEER AND WOODCRAFT.—
Moose—Cervus Hibernicus, not Antediluvian—Caraboo—
Accidents "will happen"—Virginian Deer—Toggery for the
Woods—Snow-Shoes—" Mal à la raquette" prevented—
Hints—Woodcraft—Lose way—Escape being frozen 159

CHAPTER VII.

NEW BRUNSWICK. — OF THE FISH AND FISHING. —
Salmon-spearing—Sturgeon and Molly Greenbaize—Shad
—Gaspereaux—Bass—Flies—The Curry-Curry, gaudy and
large, the best for North American waters—Matty Blake
and the " Yolly Buff"—Receipts for dying—Mosquito mixture   184

CHAPTER VIII.

NOVA SCOTIA.—A FORTNIGHT IN BUSH.—The Start—
Annapolis—Micmac Village—Flappers—Trout—Lakes—
Rivers—Still Waters—Tracks—Moose—The Death—
Potatoes—Indigestion—Turtle—Lampreys—Stone Pipes
—Calling the Moose—Emperor of China   .   . 209

CHAPTER IX.

A RACE THROUGH THE UNITED STATES.—Star-bespangled banner—Flying Artillery—Crimping System—
Table d'Hôtes—Whales and Peas—Mercantile Fowls—Sea
Speculations—Sky-blue—Yankee's Shaving—Frigid Baptists—Canals—Ontario   231

APPENDIX.

Hints to Emigrants. From Mr. Gesner's Reports on
New Brunswick   263
Average Retail Prices of Provisions and Clothing in
New Brunswick   268

Average Wages of Mechanics and others in New Brunswick 269

Of Immigration to New Brunswick . . 270

Prices of Agricultural Produce, Farming Stock, and implements of Husbandry in New Brunswick . 271

On the present state of New Brunswick in reference to a proposed Line of Railway . . . 272

On the Trees of New Brunswick . . . 280

On the Forest Trees of New Brunswick. Substance of a Lecture delivered by M. H. Perley, Esq. . . 289

" Enormous forests stretch their shadows wide,
And rich savannas skirt the mountain's side;
There bounds the moose, and shaggy bisons graze;
Scar'd by the wolf, the hardy reindeer brays;
The clambering squirrel trembles from on high,
Fixed by the rattlesnake's rapacious eye;
Unnumbered pigeons fill the darkened air,
Glut the tired hawk, the loaded branches tear;
Fair swans majestic on the waters glide,
The mason-beaver checks the flowing tide;
Gigantic rivers shake the thund'ring shore;
Dread Niagara's foaming cataracts roar;
In light canoe, the painted Indian rows,
Or hunts the floundering elk through melting snows,
Wields his huge tomahawk in deadly fray,
And rends with shouts the reeking scalp away,
Or smokes the fragrant calumet of peace,
And, bound in wampum leagues, bids savage discord cease."

ANON.

ECHOES

FROM

THE BACKWOODS.

CHAPTER I.

VOYAGE OUT.

And now there came both mist and snow,
And it grew wondrous cold:
And ice, mast-high, came floating by,
As green as emerald.

COLERIDGE.

The Transport Service — Military Life in Country
Quarters — Voyage across the Atlantic — Dense Fogs —
Banks of Newfoundland — Forests of the New World —
"The Maid of the Mist"—River St. John.

In June, 1835, the transports destined to
convey the left wing of a light infantry regiment to our colonies in North America had
" made its number" in the Cove of Cork.   At

this time the transport service was a disgrace
to the country, and, although so many men-of-
war, which might have been employed as troop-
ships, were lying idle in our numerous dock-
yards, yet the comfort of the soldiers troubled
not the heads of those gentlemen " who sit at
home at ease." It was not sufficient that the
poor devils should be "food for powder," but
that the fishes also should have their chance.
A tub of a vessel, without a sailing point in her
composition, was hired, and a mass of white
paint, in the form of a parallelogram, smeared
over her bows, the better to relieve the huge
number by which she was designated. Water-
tanks, heaps of biscuits, barrels of pork, and
but one of rum ; a pennant, an ensign, a skipper,
a fat mate, and a superannuated lieutenant of
the navy, by way of agent, and a most ina-
dequate crew, were put on board, and the
transport was reported fit for sea.[1]

[1] In the month of July, 1836, the service companies of
the Royal, or 1st Regiment, landed at Quebec " after a long

The service companies selected for duty in New Brunswick marched through Cork to the tune of " The girls we left behind us." The solemn vows of eternal constancy of the previous night were echoed and wafted from a hundred balconies ; but—

> " O, Nelly Gray ! O, Nelly Gray !
> Is this your love so warm ?
> The love that loves a scarlet coat
> Should be more uniform !"

We knew that a few hours would bring thither the new regiment, their band playing " Rory O'More," or " Sich a getting up-stairs," and that the pretty faces of the Cork fair would light up, their best bonnets would be put on, first appearances being every thing.

voyage," says Lord Charles Beauclerk in his sketch of the "Military Operations in Canada," rendered tedious from the crowded state of the ship. " In a transport of eight hundred tons, seven hundred souls were huddled together,—a number greater by far than is allowed even to vessels carrying out emigrants : and, but for the judicious arrangements of the commanding officer, malignant disease must have been the result."

Such is military life in country quarters, such is life everywhere; so—

> How happy's the soldier who lives on his pay,
> And spends half-a-crown out of sixpence [1] a day!
> He cares not a mar'vedi [2] how the world goes,
> The king finds him money, and quarters, and clothes.
> > With a row-de-dow, row-de-dow, &c.

The crowd and confusion of embarkation are not to be described : the squeaking of pigs, the quacking of ducks, the crowing of cocks, the din of French horns and kettle-drums, stray friends come to see the last of one, the curses and maledictions of the skipper, who was eventually obliged to be snubbed, and the firing off of soda-water corks, lasted until the old tub got under weigh in the most lubberly manner. Soldiers, as well as every thing else, shake into their places in a wonderfully short time ; one-third of the number are always upon deck, and are called the

[1] Sixpence was the daily pay of a British soldier previously to 1792.

[2] Maravedi, a small Spanish coin of the value of about a farthing.

watch—not that they are employed as such, but there is room only for two-thirds below. Sea-sickness was urged by many of the officers as a reason why they were not "in force;" but sundry three-cornered billets, delivered to the last weather-beaten and amphibious-looking fisher for haddocks, who boarded us when off Cape Clear, and the strict injunctions overheard as to committing them to the first post-office, induced a suspicion that to the *sea* could not be imputed *all* the sickness on board. A breeze sprung up, and, as the Emerald isle receded from view, we turned our backs upon our homes, our hunting, and our loves.

A voyage across the Atlantic, even in the best of weathers, must necessarily be a bore: calms for days; fogs, as thick as that in which the Cockney found himself enveloped when steering down Father Thames, and who requested an old tar to let him know "when they were off the Nore, for that he was very anxious to see where the mutiny had taken place."

" You are this moment abreast of it," quoth
Jack; "*but it is so thick I cannot point out
the Mutiny.*"

These fogs wet us to the skin as effectually
as the heaviest rain, and, to use a sailor's
phrase, " you might almost cut them with
a knife." Occasionally we signalized vessels,
which in return telegraphed that they should
be happy to take our letters; an insult which
had no sort of effect in hurrying our sulky
skipper. It was no object to *him* to make a
quick passage; *mais, au contraire*, the longer
he contrived to remain at sea (thanks to the
authorities) the more pay he received. What
little sail we carried was shortened at night;
and, as the fat mate generally contrived to
sleep well through his watch, no advantage
was taken of a shift of wind.

After five weeks, we were on the banks of
Newfoundland ; got soundings, but no cod;
tried to surprise turtle dozing, which proved
to be wide awake; fired at whales, and got
disagreeably near to icebergs. However, at

the end of six weeks, in spite of calms, fogs, and the sleepy mate, seas of floating kelp-weed and strong tides were met with—certain symptoms of being in or near the Bay of Fundy—and all hands looked anxiously for land. There was a dense fog; I was on deck in charge of the watch; one of the men came and reported that he saw a light, and pointed out the direction. I could not see it, but roused the fat mate, who sent men aloft, and exerted himself so far as to climb to the mizen cross-trees. I called the watch—no one could see it. The man was laughed at, but persisted in saying he distinctly saw it; he could not be drunk, for there was not the wherewithal to get so on board. Next morning's light found us close off Bryar's Island : this man *had* seen the light upon it, although invisible to sixty others.

Owing to strong tides and the prevalence of fogs, the navigation of the Bay of Fundy is ticklish in the extreme, and we felt our way by the deep sea-lead. When in stays, a large ship, unperceived until then, passed so close under our stern that a biscuit might have been thrown on her deck. She was a transport, having on board the regiment which we were going to relieve: three cheers were hardly given and returned before she was lost to sight. The fog cleared up soon afterwards, and the black masses of the pine forests of the New World opened upon us, stretching away in continued lines, until lost in distant perspective.

The first view of land, after the monotonous combination of two elements for six weeks, is exhilarating: the first sight of the primeval forests of the New World was sublime; surely such a view as this would have awakened to the power of nature even that lady's-maid who, when passing the magnificent scenery of the Via Mala, asked—from the " rumble tumble "—" Lor, how do they manage to *plant* trees in such frightful places as them there?"

On rounding a headland, the view of St.

John's broke suddenly upon us, and, from the distance, it appeared placed, as it were, in a large gap, hacked out of "the Bush." When abreast of Partridge Island, the anchor was dropped, and the transport swung to her moorings, until leave from the authorities was granted for our disembarkation. Soon after, "the Maid of the Mist"—a most appropriate name for a steamer navigating the Bay of Fundy—came alongside, and carried off a subaltern and twenty-five men to St. Andrew's, where they were to remain on detachment.

We were now within a couple of miles of the town, the largest in the province of New Brunswick. The rocky promontory upon which it stands rises from the water on all sides, and the wooden houses piled up on a series of landings give it the appearance of a fabrication made with cards to amuse children, the summit being crowned with steeples and the spires of many churches; while the base, fringed with a forest of masts, and huge ves-

sels on the stocks, proclaimed the commercial
prosperity of the place, and presented a not
unpleasing picture to our land-expecting eyes.
All hands began peering through the tele-
scopes, in hopes of getting a sight of " what
like " were the natives among whom we expected to pass the better part of three years;
and the flutter of a petticoat, or the appearance of a straw bonnet, was sufficient attrac-
tion to draw all the glasses to that spot.
The head-quarters of the regiment had arrived
a week earlier, and had been ordered up
the river St. John to Fredericton. It was
our fate to occupy the town before us. Per-
mission having at length arrived, we were
disembarked, and marched to a range of barracks pleasantly situated on a rocky promontory jutting into the harbour, and commanding the entrance of the river. No sooner
had we stowed away our men than a party of
us "Subs" rushed down into the town, hardly
checking our pace to stare at some squaws

and their papooses; nor did we stop until we arrived at a confectioner's, and obtained enormous bowls of the most delicious wood-strawberries and cream. We had just landed from a long sea-voyage; the thermometer stood at 85° in the shade; in addition to which, the woods, being on fire, made the atmosphere close and sultry; while the excitement of landing, and the bustle of putting up the men, concurred to render this the most grateful feast I ever remember to have enjoyed, and such a contrast to our ship fare, that the gluttony of the proceeding must be pardoned.

CHAPTER II.

NEW BRUNSWICK—HINTS FOR EMIGRANTS.

——Warm and buoyant, in his oily mail,
Gambols on seas of ice th' unwieldy whale;
Wide waving fins round floating islands urge
His bulk gigantic through the troubled surge;
With hideous yawn, the flying shoals he seeks,
Or clasps with fringe of horn his massy cheeks;
Lifts o'er the tossing wave his nostrils bare,
And spouts the wat'ry columns into air:
The silvery arches catch the setting beams,
And transient rainbows tremble o'er the streams.
                                    DARWIN.

First settlement of the Province—General description—
Government—Boundary question—Rivers—" The Stone
Wigwam"— Wooden Bridge — Fish — Waterfowl — The
Bore — Mineral Productions — Whales — Cod — Mines —
Divining Rod—Measures.

Those acquainted with the history of
America will no doubt remember the expedition for the discovery of heathen countries,
fitted out by Henry VII., the command of

which was intrusted to Sebastian Cabot, a
Venetian adventurer residing in Bristol. In
March, 1495, Cabot sailed from Bristol with
a small fleet, and, proceeding in a due westerly
course for some weeks, discovered a large
island, which his sailors named Newfoundland.
Thence, continuing his westerly course, he
soon fell in with another island, (now known
as Prince Edward's Island) from which he
brought off three of the natives, who conducted him across to the mainland of North
America, on which he first landed in July,
1495, somewhere between Richibucto and
Miramichi, on the northern shore of New
Brunswick. This was the first landing on
the continent of America, for it will be
remembered that Columbus did not reach the
mainland until 1498.

The English paid little attention to Cabot's
discovery, but the French very soon frequented
the Gulf of St. Lawrence in great numbers,
attracted by the excellence and extent of the
fisheries. The first permanent fishing stations

were established about 1530, within the Gulf. In 1604, an expedition sailed from France under the Sieur Des Monts, and that expedition discovered the Bay of Fundy, and the principal river of New Brunswick, the St. John, so called from its having been first entered on St. John's Day (24th June) 1604. The party of Des Monts founded Annapolis, and various fishing and trading ports were established in its vicinity. In 1625, a patent was granted by Charles I. to Sir William Alexander, afterwards Earl of Stirling, of nearly the whole of British America, and a large portion of the Northern States of the Union. Sir William made some few settlements, which existed for a short time, while various French adventurers were possessing themselves of the country, under grants from the crown of France. A constant warfare was kept up between the several settlers and claimants, until the whole country was ceded to France by the treaty of Breda, in 1667.

Nearly the whole of the territory now

known as New Brunswick was granted by the crown of France in seigneuries, between 1670 and 1688, when hostilities recommenced between England and France, and this part of America was recovered by the English. By the treaty of Ryswick, in 1696, it was again ceded to France. This peace was speedily followed by the war of the Spanish succession in 1702, during which Nova Scotia was re-conquered and permanently annexed to the British crown, but the rest of the country was ceded to France by the treaty of Utrecht in 1713. The provisions of this treaty were not fairly carried out by the French, which led to renewed hostilities; and it was not until after the taking of Louisburg and Quebec, that France relinquished all her claims to the territory by the treaty of 1763.

After the capture of Quebec, the provincial government became anxious to secure the possession of the river St. John, and to pre-vent the French from resuming possession of its fertile banks. New England had also a particular interest in the matter, as the numerous attacks upon its borders by the Indians were generally planned and fitted out by the French on the St. John.

In 1761, the Governor of Massachusetts despatched an exploring party, consisting of twelve men, under the charge of Isaac Perley, and in the pay of that State, for the purpose of ascertaining the position of affairs and the state of the country on the St. John. They proceeded from Boston to Machias by water, and then, shouldering their knapsacks, took a course through the woods, and succeeded in reaching the head waters of the Oromucto, which they descended to the St. John.

They found the country a wide waste, and no obstacles save what might be offered by the Indians to its being occupied and settled; and with this report they returned to Boston. In 1763, a party of settlers arrived from Massachusetts in four vessels in the harbour of St. John. There were about two hundred families, in all about eight hundred souls, under the charge of the same Isaac Perley. They forthwith proceeded up the St. John to Maugerville, about ten miles below Fredericton, where they established themselves, and thus made the first British settlement on the St. John. In 1765 all the country bordering on the St. John was erected into a county called Sunbury, with the province of Nova Scotia.

In 1783, in consequence of the treaty recognizing the independence of the United States, many families, who had throughout the struggle maintained their loyalty, determined to emigrate ; and in May, 1783, a large fleet, with a number of these brave spirits who had abandoned all to maintain their allegiance, arrived in the harbour of St. John. It was then a wilderness. They landed, cleared away the trees on the site of the present city, and, being joined by many others in the course of the same year, they founded the city of St. John.

On the 16th of August, 1784, a commission was issued erecting New Brunswick into a province, and appointing Thomas Carleton, Esq., the first governor ; and on the 9th of January, 1785, the first legislative assembly met in the city of St. John.

The area of New Brunswick is estimated to contain seventeen millions of acres : of these five millions of acres have been granted, two millions are deducted for water and waste, and the remaining ten millions (all fit for settlement and cultivation) remain at the disposal of the government. The population in 1824 was 74,176 ; in 1834, 119,457 ; in 1840 it was 156,162, and may now be estimated at very little short of 200,000. The government price of wilderness land is now two shillings sterling per acre, for ready money, or two shillings and sixpence, if paid by instalments in one, two, and three years, without interest.

One side of New Brunswick fronts the Bay of Fundy, the other the Gulf of St. Lawrence. It is intersected in every direction by large navigable rivers, offering great natural highways into the interior. The banks and valleys of these rivers, and their numerous tributaries, are generally very fertile, with many natural meadows, marshes, and intervals, yielding grasses spontaneously and abundantly.

The principal river is the St. John, which empties itself into the Bay of Fundy, at the city of St. John, where there is an open harbour at all seasons of the year; the St. John is four hundred miles in length, taking its rise partly in Lower Canada and partly in the United States. Fredericton, the seat of government, is eighty-four miles from the sea, on the west or right bank of the St. John. The river at Fredericton is three quarters of a mile wide, and to that place is navigated by steamers of a large class, which run up and down every day and every night—time eight hours.

The Miramichi is a large river, flowing into the Gulf of St. Lawrence; the two principal towns on this river are Newcastle and Chatham, a few miles from each other, on opposite sides, about twenty miles from the sea. Vessels of the largest class proceed to both these places to load with timber for Great Britain. Bathurst is at the mouth of the Nipisiguit, a large river flowing into the Bay of Chaleur. The country about Bathurst is yet very thinly settled, chiefly by Acadian French and Irish Catholics.

The government of the colony is modelled after that of England, having three branches. The lieutenant-governor is appointed by her Majesty; a legislative council of eighteen members, named by the crown, answer to the peers, and a legislative assembly of thirty-four members, elected by freeholders only, is an imitation of the Commons. A privy council of nine assists the governor. The members of it are appointed by the crown from the leading members of the legislative council and assembly, and hold offices during pleasure.

At the time of our arrival, and during our sojourn in the country, the disputed territory, or Boundary Question, was the all-absorbing topic. The real object of the Americans was, if possible, to substantiate such a boundary as would effectually cut off our winter communication with Quebec; and, although they have gained considerably by the final settlement under Lord Ashburton, still it is a consolation to think that they have been defeated in their main object.

As all has now been settled, the less said upon the subject the better; but it may be remarked that a line of hills divides the head waters of the rivers, which flow eastwardly into the river St. John, from those which flow towards the Penobscot river, in the State of Maine, and, as the rivers are the channels by which all the timber, the only produce of the forest, is conveyed, those hills would have therefore been the natural and most useful boundary to both parties—such a boundary as exists between the Penobscot and Milicete tribes of Indians.[1]

With the exception of the settlements at intervals upon the coasts and along the course of the principal rivers, the great mass of country may still be denominated " Bush," this said Bush containing timber of enormous growth. Birch, beech, and the rock maple, grow upon the best land; and the cunning settler marks well " the hard wood ridge," and bids for it accordingly; whereas the un-

---

[1] " Every one who has studied American affairs, even in ever so slight a degree, has in all probability been puzzled by this very boundary question. Great disgrace does and must always hang over the American Senate for the suppression of the boundary line, which was agreed to and marked out by the American minister, Benjamin Franklin, acknowledging the British claim; the discovery of this important document was made by a Mr. Sparkes, an American historian, who found it in the geological department of the Archives of France."—*Buckingham's Colonies.*

initiated emigrant is often deceived by the
healthy and flourishing appearance of the
pine tribe, and does not discover until too
late that soil which has reared such noble
timber will but ill repay him for his outlay and
trouble. That land which produces a mixed
growth of hard and soft wood is generally
supposed to be the best, when cleared, for
agricultural purposes.

The St. John, the principal river of the
province, is named by the Indians " Looshtook," which is equivalent to *Ohio*, translated
by the French, *La Belle Rivière*. It runs a
very circuitous course, winding in an irregular
semicircle, and exceeding four hundred miles
in length. In its downward course it touches
close upon the Rustigouche, to which river
there is a *portage*. The Grand Falls of the
St. John are two hundred and ten miles from
its mouth, and they constitute the greatest
fall of water east of the Mississipi, with the
exception of the Falls of Niagara. After

pursuing a southerly course, the river turns suddenly to the eastward, and contracts to half its uniform breadth. Quickening its current, it turns again suddenly to the south, and falls over a ledge of slate and limestone, seventy-four feet in perpendicular height, into a circular basin, where the water whirls round in a great eddy with resistless force.

Below the Falls, the river contracts still more, and the water is hurried over a succession of smaller falls, through a deep and rugged channel, with overhanging precipices from fifty to a hundred feet in height, for three quarters of a mile, when it is discharged into a wide basin below. The descent through this rocky channel is forty-five feet, making the total descent one hundred and nineteen feet. The water rushing through the rocky pass, as it is called, presents a scene of terrific wildness, its snowy whiteness contrasting strongly with the dark hue of the overhanging rocks and the sombre foliage of the spruce which obtains an uncertain hold in the inequalities of the precipices. Fifty miles below these falls the river becomes navigable for steamers, which, at particular seasons, reach Woodstock from St. John. Some sixty miles below Woodstock is Fredericton, the capital of the province; and the distance thence to St. John, or rather Indian Town, at the outlet of the river, is eighty-four miles.

It is curious that this magnificent river, fed by enormous tributaries and the contributions of countless lakes, after a course of upwards of four hundred miles, and an uninterrupted navigation by steamers for one hundred and forty miles of that distance, can be entered for about half an hour only in each tide by vessels of any size. The impediment arises from sunken rocks, and a steep shelf between the iron-bound gates of granite on either side, but two hundred yards apart. As soon as the flood tide has risen sufficiently to attain the level of the sunken rocks, it has to contend with the downward flood from the river. This conquered, the water for the above-mentioned short half-hour remains slack, and it is only at that time that vessels can attempt the descent.

There are pilots expressly for this passage. On one occasion, after an excursion up the river in a small yacht, I shot the rapid under the charge of one of that amphibious fraternity. The ebb had then run off but one hour, and it was anything but agreeable to witness the terrific pace at which the vessel was hurled along through the hissing eddies, now swerving and then shooting off, as if she would be dashed into a thousand pieces against the rocks; but the practised eye of the pilot, and the quickness with which she answered her helm, took us without accident clear of all danger. The pilot afterwards confessed that we had had a " narrow squeak for it," and that in ten minutes it would have been impracticable. To avoid this rapid, the steamers to Fredericton are obliged to lie just above it at Indian Town, a short mile from the town of St. John.

Great inconvenience existed from there being no bridge or other means of crossing the St. John in the immediate neighbourhood of the city; the only communication was by means of a "scow," a sort of large flat-bottomed boat, which crossed between Port-land and Carleton, a small village on the opposite side of the harbour, whence the road to St. Andrews and Fredericton branches off. The passage of this ferry in the winter was anything but agreeable, from the evapo-ration of the water when warmer than the atmosphere, with the thermometer down to a low degree. "The barber" so called is some-times so thick, that once, having embarked my sleigh to make the transit of this ferry, after some twenty minutes occupied in the operation, and after having performed four times the distance, owing to the numerous eddies in which we had been whirled about— my horses, sleigh, and furs arrived on the opposite side a complete mass of ice.

To obviate such occurrences, a Yankee conceived the bold scheme of throwing a wooden suspension-bridge across, between this ferry and the rapid above-mentioned at the outlet of the river St. John. From two enormous abutments, most ingeniously put together, he suspended his bridge, the length of which was four hundred and thirty-five feet clear of the buttresses. It had the appearance at a distance of the most beautiful lace-work—when nearly completed, and after several persons had passed over it on foot, one morning, when on parade, we heard a tremendous crash; in half an hour news arrived that the bridge had given way, and that several men were killed and many dreadfully wounded. With this smash was sunk some £30,000, the greater part of the capital

subscribed by certain enterprising share-
holders. The ruins have since been cleared
away, no attempt having been made to re-
build it.

Two steam ferry-boats however have been
established to cross the harbour, with excellent and convenient landings; four horses
may be driven on board without detaching
them from the carriage; and the distance to
Carleton on the opposite side occupies but
four minutes. These boats are not only
reported to be convenient, but I am told
profitable: the little village of Carleton
has increased rapidly since their establishment in 1839; and much of the business of
the port is now transacted on that side of
the harbour.

The Bay of Chaleur and the river Restigouche, which falls into its western extremity, separate New Brunswick from Canada.
The Bay of Chaleur is eighty-five miles long,
varying from fifteen to thirty miles in width,

and in the whole of its length and breadth
there is neither rock, reef, nor shoal. The
entrance of the Restigouche is three miles
wide, with nine fathoms water—a noble
entrance to a noble river. The Restigouche
is two hundred and twenty miles long—its
name, which is Indian, signifies " the river
which divides like the hand," in allusion to its
separation above the tide-way into five principal streams or branches. Dalhousie, at
its entrance, is a very neat town, containing
about one hundred and thirty houses, and one
thousand inhabitants. The streets are broad
and clean. In front of the town there are
some excellent wharfs, with large and well
sheltered timber-ponds. A crescent-shaped
basin and an island form an excellent harbour, where ships of any size can ride in
perfect safety.

The present extensive trade of Restigouche
sprung up about 1825, since which time
Dalhousie and Campbelltown (twenty miles

further up) have been built. The Restigouche, from Dalhousie to Campbelltown, is in
fact a harbour. Opposite to Campbelltown,
on the Canadian or Gaspé side of the river,
is Mission Point, a Micmac settlement of
about 400 souls; it is on a beautiful meadow
backed by lofty mountains, and is commonly
called by the Canadians " Le Prè du Prêtre."
The salmon-fishing on the Restigouche is very
extensive, and the fish of large size—one
establishment at Campbelltown formerly
shipped twelve hundred tierces of salmon
annually.

The length of the Miramichi, "the happy
retreat," is estimated at two hundred and
twenty miles. At its entrance into the
Gulf of St. Lawrence, it is nine miles wide,
from the north shore at Neguac to Point
Escuminac on the south. This point, as its
name, which is Indian, implies, is a long
sand-spit, with a lighthouse at its extremity,
beyond which a sandy shoal extends three

miles to seaward. The whole north-eastern coast of New Brunswick is low and sandy, and the country generally very flat, in consequence of which the tide flows for a great distance up most of the rivers. All the rivers and harbours have at their entrances sand-bars, formed by the action of the water flowing from them, on the one hand, and the heavy sea thrown in by easterly gales in the gulf on the other. There is a bar at the entrance of the Miramichi, but that river is of so large size and pours forth such a volume of water that the bar offers no impediment to navigation, there being sufficient depth of water on it at all times for ships of six and seven hundred tons.

Chatham, about twenty miles from the mouth of the river, on the south or right bank, is a busy, bustling, seaport town in the summer season, rather crowded along the water-side, which has excellent wharfs and every convenience for loading ships, the water being deep in front of the town. It contains many excellent dwelling-houses, and several large and convenient stone warehouses and stores, with every requisite for carrying on business upon a large scale. Here are extensive steam saw-mills belonging to Messrs. Cunard and Co., by whose enterprise Chatham was formed, and to whom it principally belongs. There are at this place breweries, tanneries, and founderies, built in a substantial manner on a large scale. Douglastown, on the opposite side of the river, about two miles above Chatham, is the place of business of Messrs. Gilmour, Rankin, and Co., whose plain but substantial warehouses, extensive wharfs, and well-piled deal-yards, are patterns of neatness and regularity, being admirably arranged for carrying on business extensively with the least possible amount of labour.

Newcastle, on the same side of the river as Douglastown, and three miles above it, is the shire town of Northumberland, and contains the public buildings of the county. It stands on a very level piece of ground, rising gently and gradually from the water, the court-house and churches being erected on the highest part. The streets of Newcastle are good and clean, the private dwellings plain but neat.

At the "Indian Reserve," near the Big Hole, on the north-west, is a very curious cave, which has been known to the Indians for ages; the Micmacs call the place *Condean weegan,* "the stone wigwam." Its only entrance is from the water, under a lofty overhanging cliff. The floor of the cave is about ten feet above the level of the water; the height of the uppermost overhanging ledge is seventeen feet above the floor of the cave; and the width of the entrance seventy feet. At one side of the cave, a clear and very cold spring bubbles up continually, and a natural aperture in the roof permits the smoke to escape freely; the rocks in this place are all sandstone of coarse grit, thickly studded with angular pebbles of milky and rose-coloured quartz, and the exceeding abundance of these crystals gives the place the appearance of an artificial grotto. The river rushes swiftly past the entrance, and is full of trout and salmon. The Indians spear many of the latter at this place, and they have hollowed out a basin at the spring, in which they place the salmon; and the coldness of the water keeps them fresh for two or three days.

Near Tabusintac, at Portage Island, there is a large fishing establishment of Mr. Davidson's, who has during the last three years been extensively engaged in putting up lobsters and salmon in tin cases, hermetically sealed, for foreign markets; and last season there were put up and shipped no fewer than thirteen thousand cases, each containing two pounds of salmon, or the best of three or four lobsters. The proprietor deserves great credit for his spirit and enterprise, and the poor French settlers at the Neguac villages feel the benefit of it.

At the end of September the large sea trout rush up from the gulf to the Burnt Church River preparatory to spawning, and from fifty to sixty of these may be taken with the fly on each flood tide, none of less than a pound weight.

Above Newcastle the river divides into two large branches, called the south-west and north-west Miramichi : about seventy miles up the south-west Miramichi stands Borer's Town, founded about twenty-five years since by Thomas Borer, an enterprising American, who carried on the lumber business upon a large scale and built the town. It bears a very striking resemblance to the villages in Yankee land, which spring up in the vicinity of saw-mills, being composed almost wholly of showy wooden buildings, with green Venetian and fanciful verandahs, and abundance of ornamental woodwork, not always in the best taste.

About seven miles above Borer's Town there is most excellent fly-fishing for salmon, commencing in July and ending in September. The river is frequently full of fish, and the greatest impediment to the salmon-fishing is the immense number of large trout which continually seize the salmon-flies. The trout-fishing is capital, and, in all probability, not to be excelled in any part of the world : it would astonish the fly-fishers of the mother country. Late in the season the river swarms with grilse, affording excellent sport.

At the mouth of the Miramichi, and on the whole north-eastern coast of New Brunswick, there is abundance of wild fowl of every kind. The immense flights of geese, ducks, and other migratory birds, which annually pass over to the northernmost parts of America, to breed during the summer season, remain on the coast for some time, returning to the south in

the autumn. Those who have read Audubon's
magnificent work may form some idea of the
countless thousands of birds which constitute
" a flock " on these shores ; but any attempt
at description by a less gifted pen would be
quite useless. Those only who have seen
these wonderful collections of waterfowl, and
heard their surprising clamour, can form any
idea of their extent, and, one might almost
say, grandeur—they are indeed wonderful.

The first British vessel which ever entered
the Miramichi was the frigate which conveyed the remains of Wolfe from Quebec to
England in 1759 ; that vessel, having encountered a storm in the Gulf, put in to refit, and
to obtain a further supply of water. A barge
was sent ashore for water, the whole crew
of which were barbarously murdered by the
Indians, incited, it is said, by some French
soldiers stationed at a small fort on the river.
Satisfaction, however, was taken on the spot,
for the frigate was placed abreast of the

French fort, which was soon battered to atoms. In going out of the river, the frigate was "brought up" at Burnt Church Point, all the buildings on which were battered down. A chapel, which had cost the French a sum equal to £5,000 sterling, was set on fire and wholly destroyed, whence the point has since borne the name of "Burnt Church." This point is now the property of the Micmac Indians, who have their principal settlement upon it, where they meet annually on the feast of St. Anne, (26th July) to arrange all the business of the year. They remain together about a fortnight, when chiefs are elected or deposed, marriages contracted, children baptized, and the priests who attend instruct the young in the articles of the Roman Catholic faith, to which all the Indians of New Brunswick belong.

The Tobique is one of the largest tributaries of the St. John, and flows into that river about twenty miles below the grand falls; here is a settlement of the Milicete Indians, who possess several thousand acres of excellent upland : it has been explored by Dr. Gesner. From one of his geological reports of the province, it appears that the tract of country on the shores of the Tobique, which comprehends several millions of acres, possesses most excellent soil on the uplands, and is better adapted, owing to the advantages offered by the river, to the circumstances of a respectable class of emigrants and settlers than any district in New Brunswick or Nova Scotia. The climate here is milder than it is near the coast, the mercury not rising to more than 90° Fahrenheit in the middle of the day in July. A large area in the district of the little south-west Miramichi, which flows into the Tobique, many miles above the mouth of the Wapshegan, (signifying, in the Indian tongue, " a river with a wall at its mouth,") was overrun with fires a few years ago; and the dreary appearance of this part of the country is to be attributed to that conflagration which took place about 1825 ; and the bright green forest is now reduced to a lifeless waste.

It is probable that this conflagration was the same that destroyed the towns and villages of Miramichi in October, 1825. It extended over an area of six thousand square miles, and for at least one hundred miles along the banks of the river : six hundred wretched persons perished in the flames, and a million's worth of property was destroyed. Great praise is due to the humanity shown by the people of England, who subscribed the sum of £100,000 for the relief of the sufferers ; nor was Jonathan, be it said to his credit, backward in contributing to that object.

On leaving St. John, the road to Halifax follows the line of the Kennebeckasis as far as the head-waters of the Petitcodiac, which it crosses near its source ; whence it follows the

course of that river to " the Bend," some
hundred miles from the city of St. John.
The scenery of Sussex Vale, through which this
road passes, is exceedingly fine and striking;
in many of the bogs and swamps there are
extensive deposits of bog iron ore, which
might be worked with great advantage, being
of good quality, and in the immediate neighbourhood of abundance of wood for fuel;
and its proximity to the Westmoreland coal
field ought to be a further inducement to
engage in its manufacture. The bogs also
abound in the brown, yellow, and red oxides
of iron, which will afford ochres for pigments.

The river Petitcodiac is navigable for vessels of one hundred tons for thirty-three
miles from its mouth, and the tide flows
inland some six and thirty; but the most
extraordinary feature of the river is " the
Bore," Dr. Gesner's account of which is so
interesting, that it must be its own apology
for its introduction. " At the Bend," writes

that gentleman, " the stream, having entered
from the south, turns suddenly to the westward, at the distance of twenty miles from
its mouth. At this place the tide flows in
and ebbs off in six hours, running at the rate
of seven miles per hour. The flood tide is
accompanied by a tidal wave called the *bore*,
which at high tides is five, and sometimes six
feet high. The rushing of this overwhelming
wave produces a noise like that of a number
of steamboats in operation, and is one of the
most interesting spectacles the country affords.
The salmon and shad, urged forward by the
sweeping current, to avoid the force of the
stream, seek the shallow water near the
shores, where they are discovered by their
wake, chased by wading sportsmen, and fairly
caught.

" At low water, extensive flats are laid
bare ; these are composed of fine shingle and
quicksands, which, with the *bore* and rapid
tide, have been the cause of several ship-

wrecks. The danger to vessels arises from
venturing too early on the flood and too late
on the ebb tide. In the first instance, they
overrun the tide, and are stranded in the
quicksands; in the second, the tide leaves
them before they arrive in deep water.
When thus situated, if they resist the fury
of the *bore*, the water washes the sand away
from the leeward side: they roll over before
the current, breaking their masts, and, finally,
filling with shingle, they are buried in a
sandy grave. The *bore* is much higher and
more violent in some parts of the river than
in others, a circumstance probably arising
from the configuration of the shore and the
bottom of the river.

" At the Bend there is a considerable village. The soil is chiefly of two kinds, the
sandy and the clayey. Lime, if judiciously
applied, would greatly improve both varieties, and the admixture of marsh and mud
would increase the fertility of fields where

the clay is absent. There are large tracts of marsh on each side of the Petitcodiac, of which a portion has been diked, and is under cultivation.

' The northern side of the coal district in this quarter was observed about ten miles from the entrance of the Petitcodiac.

" Coal appears on both sides of the Meram- cook river, the Petitcodiac river, and ten miles north of Shepody. The whole length of the coal field of Westmoreland is upwards of seventy miles; its average breadth, esti- mating the area on each side of the Petitco- diac, is about seventy miles.

" At Slack's Cove and Drake's Cove excel- lent grind-stones are obtained from the nume- rous strata of sand-stone which there abound, and are the best stones for cutting and polishing metals hitherto found in America. The reefs are broken at low water, and masses of rocks are secured to large boats; at high water they are brought to the shore, where they are cut by the workmen with great facility into grinding stones from four to eight feet in diameter, and from six inches to a foot in thickness. These are called 'water stones,' and are extensively used in the United States, for grinding down and polishing all kinds of cutlery. Other grindstones of less dimensions are made from the rocks situated above the tide; these are used for common purposes—the price of each stone delivered on the shore is from two to three shillings: they are sold in the United States from six shillings and threepence to nine shillings per stone. The trade is therefore profitable.

"The Shediac coast is famous for its oysters, which are so abundant that the inhabitants make use of their shells for manure. The harbour of Shediac is safe and convenient for vessels of large size; but it is a curious fact that the numerous beds of oysters along these coasts are constantly lessening the depth of the sea, and gradually filling up the bays. Lime prepared from these oyster-shells is reported to have great effect when applied to the light and sandy soil along this line of coast, and to render it very fertile."

In the neighbourhood of Fort Cumberland and the Tantamar Marshes there is excellent snipe-shooting, but the improvements and draining at present in progress will in a few years convert all into the richest land. The country about is very fine, and a brother officer described it as well worth a visit. He drove his horses from Halifax to Windsor, Kentville, Amherst, and back by Truro, and during his trip contrived to bag six hundred and fifty head of snipe and woodcocks.

There are large tracts of peat in every part of New Brunswick wherever there is low ground : this is occasioned by the decay of mosses that are always found to flourish in low lands. This peat is valuable for fuel, but at present it is not necessary to use it for such a purpose, owing to the vast quantity of timber: however, by skilful management it may be converted into excellent manure.

In many places there are to be found beds of excellent clay of different colour, which are adapted for making bricks; and Nature has been bountiful enough to place strata of sand beneath these beds, thereby affording to man an easy way of providing for his comfort in many respects; for, without the sand, the clay would not answer for burning. In addition to a great supply of mineral ores, and the climate being such as to produce the most luxuriant growth of grain, according to official returns, 3,634,280 acres have been already granted to applicants for land in New Brunswick, and 13,792,272 remain still at the disposal of the Crown. Out of this quantity of land 440,000 acres are cleared, but there are about 12,000,000 acres capable of immediate cultivation. The land in the southern part of the province is not near so well adapted to agricultural purposes as in the other parts.

The district of Gaspé is an extensive peninsula, about ninety miles in width from the Bay of Chaleur to the Gulf of St. Lawrence, with a coast line of two hundred and fifty miles from Cape Chat to the Restigouche. Gaspé Basin, which lies between Cape Gaspé and Whale Head, runs about sixteen miles into the land, and is about five miles broad. This place is considered one of the best and safest harbours in America; being capable of containing three hundred sail of vessels in perfect security.

The inhabitants of Gaspé Basin are nearly all fishermen, most of whom are exclusively employed about the whale fishery. They fit out every season four or five schooners, of seventy or eighty tons each, manned with ten or twelve men, who are engaged in whaling during all the summer months. The fishery yields about twenty thousand gallons of oil annually, which is sent to Quebec for a market, and gives employment to about two hundred men.

The whales are of the species called "Humpbacks," and yield about three tons of oil each, but some of them have been taken of the length of sixty or seventy feet, yielding eight tons of oil. Each schooner has two whale-boats, with the usual outfit of harpoons, lines, and lances. The whales swim fast and are very shy. They appear off the entrance of Gaspé Basin in the spring, and the whalers follow them during the summer to the Island of Anticosti and the north shore of the St. Lawrence, a wild and desolate region, frequented by a singular race of Indians, known to the Canadians as "Les Montagnards," or the Mountaineers. They are supposed to be the last of the Algonquins.

This settlement in Gaspé Basin was formed in 1764 by Felix O'Hara, Esq., late judge of

the district of Gaspé, who emigrated from
Ireland, and was the first person that settled
in Gaspé for agricultural purposes. He was
most deservedly and highly esteemed.

The cod-fish caught and cured on the
shores of Gaspé are generally of small size,
but are much liked in foreign markets, from
their being well preserved. This arises from
the fish being caught near the shore, and
being split and salted while perfectly fresh
and firm. The process of cleaning the fish
is carried on in a very neat and expedi-
tious manner. The boats, as soon as they
return from the fishing-bank, run alongside
a stage, which is built over the water, on
which they are thrown out. The first man
who handles the fish cuts the throat with a
single stroke of his knife; then he slides it
along a sort of table to another, who whips
off the head, and drops it, with the entrails,
through a hole in the table into the water
beneath, retaining only the liver, which is

thrown into a tierce to make oil. The next
man splits the fish, and takes out the bone;
and on the manner in which these operations
are performed, in a great degree depends the
quality of fish for market.

When split, the fish are carried to a large
covered building, where, after being well
washed, they are rubbed with salt, and placed
in little flat piles on the floor to drain; after
being sufficiently struck with salt, they are
carried out to the Shingle Beach to dry, or,
where there is no beach, are spread on long
narrow wicker frames, or stages set up for the
purpose. The labour of spreading and turning
the fish is incessant and severe : they require
to be frequently turned to prevent their being
scorched by the sun or salt-burnt. The
person who turns does so in a systematic
manner, with his right and left hand alter-
nately; so that not one fish in thousands may
be missed.

After the fish are sufficiently cured, they

are collected and laid in small circles with the tails outwards; these circles are continually built upon, each row being larger than the one below it, until the pile is about three feet high, when the circles begin to diminish, so as to form a conical roof; this is covered with birch-bark, and stones are laid upon it. The piles are thus rendered impervious to the heaviest rains, and in this position the fish are left to season before being packed for exportation. The bait used for cod are herring and the caplin, a peculiar little fish, which when dried, is considered a great luxury for the table. In the latter part of the season, when other bait becomes scarce, clams are used, and the fishermen complain that they frequently have more labour and undergo more fatigue in procuring bait, than in taking the cod afterwards.

The state of the law and the administration of justice in Gaspé have caused much discontent for some time past, and commissioners were sent from Quebec last year to report the true state of matters.

In Gaspé there are not only lead mines, but also extensive beds of coal, not existing in geological reports, but actually to be found and worked. A company has been lately established in London by royal charter, for the purpose of carrying on the fisheries and working the mines of Gaspé.

The agricultural district of Gaspé may be said to commence at New Carlisle. To the westward the land is not only better, but the inhabitants are less devoted to fishing and more to farming.[1]

In all countries, however civilized, amongst some of its inhabitants there will be found a strong superstitious belief in divination, practised more or less by some of its votaries. This is the case in New Brunswick, and an absurd belief in the powers of divination prevails to a great extent. A system ori-

[1] For further particulars see Appendix.

ginally to be traced to the Druids, to awe their superstitious followers, called " the mineral or divining rod," has been introduced into the province from the eastern American States, and has found votaries among persons otherwise intelligent. The power of divination is supposed to be contained in two small phials fixed on pieces of whalebone, and borne by the seventh son of a seventh son. This is the person who alone can be successful, and is always supposed to be infallible. This rod is used for the purpose of discovering concealed money and all kinds of minerals; even in places where they have no real existence, except in the mind of the infatuated. Much the same sort of superstitious belief exists in Ireland, where they listen to the supposed dreams of some old hag, who declares that in her sleep she has been informed of the identical spot where in some " rath" is to be found the " *crock of gould*" so much sought after by the *pisantry.*

The measures of length, surface, and weight, are the same as in England; the measures of capacity, the same as in England before the introduction of the imperial measure.

The rate of exchange with Britain is fixed by estimating the Spanish dollar at 5s. currency, and 4s. 6d. sterling; but the actual rate of exchange is 24s. currency for the sovereign. To bring sterling to currency, add one fifth; to bring currency to sterling, deduct one sixth.

CHAPTER III.

NEW BRUNSWICK.—CONTINUED.

The ice was here, the ice was there,
        The ice was all around;
It crack'd and growl'd, and roar'd and howl'd,
        Like noises in a swound!
                    COLERIDGE'S *Ancient Mariner*.

Towns—Labrador dogs—Horse-dealing—Cobbett—
Agent for "Morrison's pills"—A fire—Amusing incident—
Climate—Lumber, hard and soft wood—Below *Nero*—
Effects of frost—Skating—Sleighing—Coasting—Sleigh
Club—Corn-bin extraordinary—Perilous situation.

Fredericton, the capital of the province, is
built on an extensive plain encircled by a
range of high lands in the rear, which rises
from the river at the lower extremity of the
plain, and closes in to the river above, leaving
a level space, nearly four miles long, and a
mile wide at the broadest part. The river
forms a beautiful curve around this plain;

and near the centre of the town, at what was
formerly called St. Ann's Point, there is a
fine view of the river Nashwaak, which falls
into the St. John directly opposite. The
high grounds which surround Fredericton form
a beautiful steeply inclined plane, on which
several public and private buildings have been
erected. King's College, on the acclivity of
this hill, is 171 feet long, and 59 feet wide,
with projections; it has a massive cornice
with pediment; and the principal material
of the building is the dark gray stone found
near its site. It consists of a basement with
two lofty stories; contains twenty rooms for
students, with the necessary accommodations
for the principal professors, attendants, and
servants. The situation of the college is
healthy, and commands a fine view of the
town and adjacent country. To the eastward, there is a full view of the river and
the surrounding country, as far as the
Oromucto.

A bishop has lately been appointed to New
Brunswick, and Fredericton has been con-
stituted an episcopal city. The erection of a
cathedral, to cost £30,000, has just been
commenced. Fredericton is 84 miles from
St. John. Steamers perform the distance in
eight hours; and, when the river becomes
frozen, it forms, for the greatest part of the
way, the sleigh-track between the two cities.

When approached by water from St. John,
the quiet and rural situation of this comparative village is most pleasing. The river, here
three quarters of a mile in width, glides
smoothly, silently, and unruffled, past the
neat wooden range of barracks, with their
grassplot and fine old weeping willows, under
the broad shade of which, in the cool evening
of the Indian summer, the ladies of Fredericton
may listen to soft music. On the slope of
the range of hills behind the town, King's
College, with its roof of iron, shines resplendent in the sunshine; and, on the opposite

side of the river, the blue smoke from the
wigwams of the Indians curls up in wreaths
against the dark line of the pine forest, and,
reflected in the glassy surface of the river,
presents a picture of perfect repose. On the
day on which I first approached it, the heat
and mirage gave it that appearance only to
be seen in the best works of the inimitable
Claude.

Government House is placed some three
quarters of a mile up the river, on the same
side as the town; it is a handsome stone
building of three stories, with wings and a
semicircular portico, in a pleasant park and
near the banks of the river. In few of the
colonies are the governors more commodiously
or comfortably housed than in New Brunswick;
and no expense has been spared of late years
in furnishing and perfecting the house and
grounds. At this time, the amateurs of the
Labrador dog might have been gratified to
see sixteen or eighteen of this noble breed

rush into the water, and contend for the
Governor's prize—his walking-stick. They
were of the true sort, with fine intelligent
countenances; and when they emerged from
the river, the water ran from their silky
and jet-black coats as from a tarpauling
covering.

Some twelve miles below Fredericton is the
town of Oromucto, situated on the mouth of
the river of that name, where it joins the
St. John. In New Brunswick they have had
the good taste in general to preserve the
Indian names of the rivers, which invariably
express their character. Thus the "Oromucto" signifies "the deep rolling river;"
the "Washadamoak," which is passed lower
down, is the "River of Rapids," and the
"Beggaguimmick," a stream above Fredericton, is the "Dancing Stream," the "Richibucto," the "River of the Burnt Country,"
&c., &c. It is a thousand pities ever to
change such names for such as are compre-

hended in the vile catalogue from which the Yankees generally contrive to select the most inappropriate.

Opposite to Gagetown, a small village 30 miles below Fredericton, is the Gemseg, or outlet of the Grand Lake ; and lower down is " The Mistake," a long creek, the entrance to which is of equal width with the main stream, and has so much the appearance of being the channel of the river, that few are they who have made the upward trip in either sail or row boat but have, after a long sail or a tough row, discovered the end of the deceitful creek, and been obliged to return to the main stream.

The scenery of St. John is decidedly fine : on either side alluvial meadows of the richest soil produce fine hay crops; and, like the valley of the Nile, are regularly " top-dressed" by the periodical floods of the river. Further down is found the entrance to Belleisle Bay, where the winter road from St. John debouches upon the river, whence it follows its course on the ice to Fredericton. Occasionally a large vessel is seen on the stocks in the numerous lateral creeks or still waters off the main river. From the junction of the Nerepis with the St. John, the latter expands into a fine sheet of water. The bay of Kenebekasis opens on the left—that passed, the channel of the river becomes again confined by bold rocks, fringed with spruce firs: here and there an Indian wigwam peeps from among them, while an occasional birch canoe, silently and cautiously paddled along shore, contrasts its gay cargo of gaudy-coloured workmanship with the dark shadows of the firs, and gives a picturesque finish to the long course of the river St. John, or " Looshtook."

On the 18th day of May, 1783, the first of a sturdy band of loyalists landed upon the rocky peninsula where now stands the city of St. John. It was then covered with a dense and tangled forest, and the first comers cleared away the trees and underwood only sixty-two years since, from a spot of ground now covered with costly buildings, and daily thronged with eager crowds, busily engaged in carrying on a thriving, prosperous, and extensive trade. From this small beginning a city has sprung up, which, with its suburbs, now numbers nearly 30,000 inhabitants, and carries on a large business with all parts of the world; and even before the roots of the trees which were cut down by the loyalists have rotted away, or their toils and privations have ceased to be a subject of conversation, *there* is to be found every means and appliance of refinement and luxury, and all the substantial comforts of modern days.

The city stands on rugged, rocky, and uneven plots of ground; but, within a few years, large sums have been expended in levelling and filling up, so that the streets now present excellent thoroughfares, inclined on easy slopes. St. John, being an incorporated city,

is governed by a mayor, recorder, six aldermen, and six assistants, under the style of
" The Mayor, Aldermen, and Commonalty of
the city of St. John." The mayor, recorder,
common clerk, sheriff, and coroner, are appointed by the governor. The aldermen and
assistants are chosen annually by the free-
men of the city.

The port of St. John is convenient and
safe, and sufficiently spacious to accommo-
date a great number of vessels. The ebb
and flow of the tide is from twenty-four to
thirty feet perpendicular; and one of the most
important advantages of the harbour is, that
in the most severe winter it is free of ice.

Within the harbour is a valuable fishery:
several thousand barrels of gaspereaux are
taken annually, with many thousand salmon
and shad. The salmon are now sent by the
steamers, packed in ice, to Boston, where
they fetch high prices; and this fishery has
become exceedingly valuable.

The imports into St. John consist chiefly of British manufactures and colonial produce; the exports are lumber, fish, furs, oils, and lime, masts, spars, and other timber.

Ships of a fine class are built here of the spruce and birch of the country: they sail well, look smart and taunt on the water, and, although not in general treated to copper, answer the purpose for which they have been built. From the Bays of Miramichi and Chaleurs, Chinecto and St. Andrew's, besides bays and rivers too numerous to specify, are launched others equally fine. Here, as in Holland, the stranger is often surprised to come suddenly upon a huge vessel, constructing in the settler's kitchen-garden, to launch which he has to trust to his own ingenuity, and to Providence for a deluge.

Besides the steamers which ply on the river, between St. John and Fredericton, there is steam communication to Annapolis and Windsor in Nova Scotia, to St. Andrew's and

Eastport in the State of Maine and the Bay
of Passamaquoddy; and, during the time we
were stationed at St. John, a fine boat, the
Royal Tar, was built to run to Portland, in
the United States. Unluckily, when on her
third or fourth trip, she took fire and burnt
to the water's edge. On board was a large
menagerie of wild beasts, all of which were
either burnt or drowned, with the exception
of an elephant, which contrived to get clear of
the vessel and swim to land; much to the
astonishment of some of the Penobscot Indians, attracted to the shore by the sight of
the vessel in flames. The " Sea Serpent "
case has puzzled Europeans; what could have
astonished the red men more than to see a
huge animal of whose existence they knew
nothing swimming lustily to shore? Sir
Humphrey Davy's opinion of this supposed
monster is decidedly the best which has been
adduced: he says—" The Sea Snakes seen by
American and Norwegian captains have, I

think, generally been a company of porpoises, the rising and sinking of which in lines would give somewhat the appearance of the coils of a snake." Such is Sir H. Davy's opinion of the Sea Serpent, and not a bad one either.

The merchants of St. John are most enterprising, and great fortunes are often made in a very short time—sometimes lost in much less. It is said that to a successful haul of herrings may be traced the rise of the richest man in the province. They will embark in any probable speculation—witness the Suspension Bridge over the river St. John; no sooner proposed by a cunning Yankee, than £20,000 were instantly forthcoming. A tinge of the Yankee occasionally appears amongst innkeepers and that class of men. I once wrote to "mine host" of a tavern kept in St. John to inquire what price he put upon a neat gray horse, which he possessed, and which I was anxious to buy for a leader in my sleigh. I received the following laconic answer :—

"Mr. Scoales will not take less than £25 for his gray horse till he alters his mind."

The streets of St. John are laid out regularly, and at right angles. King's Square, at the top of the town, I have seen filled with the militia of the district; as fine and as loyal a body of men as any in her Majesty's dominions. In the late war, the 104th Regiment or New Brunswick Fencibles, were raised here, sent over the Portage to Quebec on snow-shoes, and did good service for the mother country. The original settlers of St. John were, as before stated, loyalists, who left the United States when they obtained their Independence, and raised the few fishing-huts which then stood in " Bush " into the city of St. John. At the same time, many negro families arrived, who are still located in the " back slums."

As to " lions," they must of necessity be few. The house inhabited by Lord Edward Fitzgerald is still standing—a mere log hut, by

comparison with the smart houses built by the
present generation. Cobbett was stationed
here, and married a wife who lived on Fort
Howe Hill. He says in some of his writings
that he fell in love with her (as he was going
to parade) at the door of a small log hut,
where she was busily employed in scrubbing
the milk-pails. He was sergeant-major in the
same regiment with Lord Edward; and wrote,
when stationed here, a clever treatise on the
tides and navigation of the Bay of Fundy.

The greatest living curiosity, at the time I
was stationed there, was the agent for " Morrison's Pills." That compounder of bread
and gamboge, and prince of quacks, had most
judiciously selected the fattest and most
healthy-looking commercial ambassador to
puff off his concoctions; and a peep at the
bloated charlatan must have been the strongest
recommendation to the efficacy of his me-
dicine.

At the time of our arrival, the town of St.

John was built almost entirely of wood, and had the bad luck to be burnt down, more or less, every four or five years; and that part which escaped one conflagration was generally included in the next. At this time there existed but one house—with the exception of the banks—built of stone, the inhabitants of which were known as the Stonehouse P——s, the better to distinguish them from their wooden connexions.

One night after mess, a messenger arrived from the mayor, stating that a fire had broken out in the town. A strong armed piquet was instantly despatched: scarcely had they left the barracks, before a second messenger made his appearance, reporting that fears were entertained lest the whole town would be consumed. All hands then turned out, and went down at the " double march." It blew a gale of wind. The thermometer stood at 7° below zero, the fire raged, every thing was frozen up, and no water was to be obtained, except in the immediate neighbourhood of the wharfs. The scene of confusion was beyond description. Gentlemen, either from over-excitement or inebriation, floundered into tar-barrels, took fire, and rushed about requesting to be extinguished; one had, partly from the above cause, partly from fatigue, sat down in a wheelbarrow on one of the quays; it was within the influence of a hose, the spray from which, aided by 39° of frost below the freezing point, soon made him part and parcel of the barrow. A friend found him, and no one being at hand, he was wheeled off to be cut out.

To the ladies it appeared the greatest possible fun, throwing beds, wardrobes, and all their finery out of the windows, and trusting to friends to carry them to the banks or other places of safety. On the part of the authorities of the town, there was neither order, system, nor regularity observed; it was every one for himself, and the soldiers for them all.

In the hope of cutting off the fire, grappling-
hooks with long ropes attached to them were
thrown over houses, and by the force of a
hundred men pulled bodily down. The officers
and men worked like horses. But all was to
no purpose :

> The grappling-hook plucks rafters from the walls,
> And heaps on heaps the smoky ruin falls.
> Blown by strong winds, the fiery tempest roars,
> Bears down new walls, and pours along the floors.

The fire raged unchecked, as ashes and burning shingles were carried by the wind, and
fresh houses and streets ignited. Notwithstanding the flames and the exertion of the
men, so intense was the cold, that many of
them were frost-bitten.

All hopes of extinguishing the fire being
abandoned, one of the authorities sent to the
commanding-officer, requesting that guards
might be despatched to the different roads leading out of the town; for that sleigh-loads of
plunder (the bells being taken off the horses to

enable them to get away unheard) were carried
off, and boats were employed by sea for the
same purpose. I proceeded with the picquet
to one of the roads; the cold was so severe
that we were obliged to run up and down to
keep the blood in circulation, and had not
enjoyed this jog-trot exercise long, when the
sergeant reported that an unnaturally fat
woman was coming along, and at a very slow
pace, considering the state of the atmosphere;
hinting, at the same time, at some comparisons
with a lady of Carlton (on the other side of the
river), who a few days previously had blessed
the province with four little Bluenoses [1] at
one birth. She was examined, and *safely
delivered* of quantities of plunder, which she
had swathed round her body.

Alongside of the South Market Wharf lay
a tier of vessels, and, some powder having ex-
ploded, the one nearest to the wharf was in

[1] All persons born in the provinces of Nova Scotia and
New Brunswick are called Bluenoses.

imminent danger. An inhabitant of the town, Mr. W———, went up to Corporal Harrison, who, with a party of the regiment, had saved upwards of two hundred casks of spirits on the said wharf—and slapped him on the back —" Corporal," said he, " we are not afraid of a little powder."—" No," replied Harrison— " nor a great deal of fire either."

The heat had by this time become so intense as to set fire to the fore-topsail of the brigantine—and a second explosion almost immediately took place. All hands then left the vessels to their fate, and all of them must have perished, had it not been for the gallant conduct of the above mentioned Corporal Harrison and private John Burgess, who went aloft, and by means of the signal-halliards, with a bucket attached to each end, managed to keep the sails sufficiently wet to stay the progress of the flames and to prevent further mischief. The tide then began to make, and a boat with some sailors came to their assistance : a rope was made fast to the wharf, and the vessels were hauled clear of the fire and further damage.

Corporal William Harrison and Private John Burgess, for their daring conduct on this occasion, were presented with the freedom of the city of St. John.   Quere, would they not have benefited much more by a ten pound note?

Towards daybreak the fire was at its greatest pitch.   Numbers of casks, filled with oil and blubber, took fire.   The effect was sublime, and the liquid sheet of flame was seen for sixty miles in all directions.[1]

[1] By this fire, which broke out on the 14th of January, 1837, and consumed 115 houses and stores, many of them valuable and full of merchandize, more than one-third of the " business " part of the city, containing buildings and property to the amount of £250,000, was swept away. In August, 1839, another destructive fire swept off about 200 buildings, likewise in the business part of the city ; and these two great fires have been followed by others of less amount. The erection of wooden buildings is now prohibited by law ; many massive ranges of stone and brick at present occupy the places of the old wooden shanties, and the town wears an altogether different appearance.

Notwithstanding the changes from extreme heat to intense cold, the climate of New Brunswick is particularly healthy. The summers are fine ; fogs occasionally prevail at St. John, and in the immediate neighbourhood of the Bay of Fundy. The autumn (so expressively termed " the fall ") is delightful, particularly the two latter months known as " the Indian summer," at which time the early frosts tinge the leaves of the hard wood with the brightest colours imaginable. The effect of this varied foliage, of every shade of yellow, scarlet, and purple, when contrasted with the deep greens of the fir tribe, is striking in the highest degree, and can only be compared to a painter's pallet, or a modern picture of " *La Jeune France* " school. This season is most enjoyable, and the sunsets are glorious. About Christmas the snow has fallen, and the frost may be said to have fairly set in. The sun shines bright and clear in the deep blue heavens. Though the thermometer

may be down to five-and-twenty degrees below
zero, there is something particularly exhilarating in the dry, clear air. The nights are
proportionably fine, and the northern lights
may be seen in all their glory, often assuming
that beautiful rose colour nowhere to be wit-
nessed so grand as in the northern latitudes.

Then the lumberers repair to the backwoods
in search of the pine and spruce fir, which
grow to enormous heights, often two hundred
feet, perfectly straight and healthy, and so
close together as to be self-pruned; a knife
should never be applied to any of the fir tribe
(a pernicious practice too often perceptible in
English plantations), it only causes the tree
to bleed. The axes of the American lumberers are totally different from those used in
the old world. The haft, made of hickory,
is curved, and has a knob at the end; in de-
livering the stroke, the axe is swung as high
as the head, the hands slipping up to the knob.
Two backwoodsmen will fell one of these huge

pines in an incredibly short time. Of course
when a tree is thus cut breast high, in addition
to perhaps three feet of snow upon which the
man may have been standing, there is a
waste of timber which, although not thought
of in the forests of America, would be a serious consideration in England. When felled
and snagged, one end of the tree is placed
upon a small sleigh, and dragged out of the
bush by oxen. It is then piled along with
others upon the frozen rivers, and the mass is
carried down by the stream when the ice
breaks up; passing in its progress through
lakes, and from river to river, till it reaches
the St. John, where the logs are claimed by
their different owners, formed into rafts, and
finally descend to St. John, whence they are
shipped for England.

A propos to timber, it is a curious fact
that, in the forests of North America, should
the primeval growth be hard wood, oak, beech,
birch, hickory, maple, &c., and be cut down *en*

masse, pine or firs spring up in their stead, and *vice versâ :* further, should the second growth be allowed sufficient time to attain any size, the same effect will ensue on felling that, and so *ad infinitum.* The same thing may be observed in the forests of Carniola and Bohemia ; it is the case in all natural forests, and was also remarked by Franklin in the sterile districts inhabited by the Esquimaux.

The cold during the winter nights is very severe. The sentinels are frequently obliged to be relieved every half hour, and the officers, so long as they are beardless, may enjoy horizontal refreshment in peace ; but when they obtain those manly appendages, yclept whiskers, they find that turning in bed becomes hopeless, and, being " brought up with a round turn," discover that they are frozen to the sheets ; and we were told that families have been awakened by their house becoming roof-less, owing to the intensity of the frost having extracted the nails by which the shingles were fastened to the rafters. Provisions are brought into St. John frozen hard, and they will keep perfectly well so long as the frost lasts; it is ludicrous enough to see pigs, hares, and large cod-fish frozen stiff, and carried by a leg or tail over a man's shoulder like a musket.

One evening a discussion as to the degree of cold led to a bet, and the commanding officer's orderly was sent to ascertain what the thermometer stood at outside the window. The major's servant ingenuously brought the thermometer into the room, and looked at it by the light of the fire; the mercury, thus suddenly astonished, naturally ran up at a tremendous pace. In the conversation which took place between him and the orderly he was overheard exclaiming, " Wait till it stops, Bob! Now, tell the major it is at forty-five notches above *Nero*."

Skating, sleighing, and dancing are the amusements of the opulent; so anxious were some of the young ladies to make their *debút*,

E 5

that at one of the balls a fair creature, whom
the morning's *lecon* had advanced only to the
third figure of the quadrilles, stood up to
dance with a brother officer; on arriving at
l'été, she deliberately walked off, and returned
to her place, exclaiming, "Now I guess I'll
sit down; I don't know any more," leaving her
partner to make his peace with her *vis-à-vis*.

Yachting on the frozen Kenebekasis was
but a frigid amusement at the best. The
manufacture of an ice-boat is simple enough :
over two long skates are placed any construction sufficient to hold the party, and a long
pole is lashed across at right angles, which
prevents the boat from capsizing. When the
wind is high, she flies over the ice at a most
terrific rate; and goes so near the wind, that
the least touch of the helm sends her round,
when she is instantly off again on the other
tack. A favourite amusement is coasting.
On moonlight nights, a party repair to the
top of some steep frozen descent, and ladies

and gentlemen in pairs seat themselves upon little sleighs or coasters, and push them off. After a thaw the frost makes the surface of the snow as slippery as glare ice; the pace is then awful, and the roll in the snow proportionate. They are steered in their headlong descent by a slight pressure of the heel; but the Bluenose ladies, being more *au fait* at it than we were, sat in front and guided them.

The meeting of the Tandem Club was a very gay affair; twice in each week, twenty sleighs, painted of the most gaudy colours, and decked out with furs of all kinds, trimmed with fringe of different colours, drove off from the barracks or other rendezvous. The last married lady was selected as chaperon, and there were plenty of fair candidates for the drive. The brass band and merry bells added not a little to the cheerfulness of the scene.

The sleighs used in New Brunswick are of all forms and kinds—from that constructed with a couple of ash-poles (a nick alone dis-

tinguishing where the runners terminate and
the shafts commence) with a few boards placed
across to support a barrel, in which the victim
sits or stands, to the double or single sleighs
on high runners, not forgetting the Madawaska
Cariole, the height of luxury and the perfection of locomotion, and in which you recline,
covered up to the chin in furs. It is absolutely necessary in the construction of a
sleigh that the "runners" should be a good
distance apart, and "flare out" sufficiently;
for, should the road be covered with ice and
"bogged up" in the centre, the sleigh will
slide to one side with great velocity, particularly when turning a corner sharp. This
is called "*slewing*," and the slightest impediment on the ice will then be sufficient to upset
the sleigh. When a "slew" takes place, it is
necessary to pull the shaft-horse *with it;* a
beginner is sure to do exactly the reverse, and
is certain to be capsized. Even a high wind
is sufficient to blow a sleigh round in an ex-

posed situation, and upon " glare ice," when an upset is likely to happen, unless the runners " flare out" well at bottom.

I originally purchased a sleigh with faulty runners; and had several upsets and smashes, on which occasions the wreck alone of the " conveyance" reached barracks. One day, out sleighing on the Kenebekasis, the ice was glare, and in the most perfect order: there was not the slightest draught, and my horses were trotting along merrily at the rate of twelve miles an hour, when, all at once, a squall of wind caught the sleigh and spun it round; and the runners at the same time encountering some roughness on the surface, the sleigh was upset, and the horses, as is generally the case, instantly set off at full gallop; for some time I was held in by the apron, and slipped along on my side, keeping a tight hold of the reins. The leader was galloping like a Caraboo, and the shaft-horse giving occasional kicks at the mass of encum-

brance about his heels. At length the apron
gave way, and, still holding on by "the
ribbons," I was jerked off in the manner of
one of those swings used in gymnastic acade-
mies, to be as quickly banged against the
splash-board; and, four or five of these *coups*
coming in quick succession, I was obliged to
shorten my hold of the reins, and, the distance between the shaft-horse's heels and my
head being in consequence much diminished,
I thought with the knight "that discretion
was the better part of valour," and—let go.

On getting up and shaking myself, I saw
my servant, who had been pitched out of the
hind seat, some three quarters of a mile
behind, and the distance between him and
myself preserved in perspective by sundry
cushions, skins, linings, and bits of fringe;
and, on turning to look after the sleigh, I had
the felicity to see the horses still going
" Derby pace," and just debouching from the
ice, "steering wild" for a gap in a "zigzag"

fence. Bang they went against the rails, giving the *coup de grace* to the proceeding, and going well away into the woods with the shafts dangling about their heels. I *then* built a new sleigh.

The painting and trimming up of the sleigh depend much upon the taste of the possessor; the general colours are dark bodies, with scarlet runners. I found that a white ground, picked out with bright vermilion, and bear and buffalo skins, with a liberal quantity of deep scarlet curtain fringe, and scarlet cloth, cut into scallops, arranged in studied confusion, the whole furnished with a huge pair of moose-horns in front, looked extremely light and gay on the snow; and the white, from being relieved by the vermilion, had no dirty appearance when contrasted with the snow.

The horses bred in the province are compact little animals, and trot at a tremendous pace, particularly upon glare ice; so docile

are they, from being brought up in the house
as part of the family, and so attached are the
Bluenoses to them, that a man, hearing I possessed a gray horse (a famous trotter) which
he had bred, came a long distance to see him.
Two years had elapsed since he had sold him;
he might have been " *a whisperer;*" but no
sooner had he entered the stables, and spoken
to him, than the horse reared upon his hind-
legs, and showed every symptom of recognition
and delight.   I drove that horse and another,
without the least preparation, from St. John
to Fredericton in ten hours; the ice was in
good order; the distance eighty-four miles.
An officer of the 52nd made a match against
a stage-driver, a noted character in the province, to perform the same distance.   One of
the driver's horses dying from over-exertion,
the gallant captain was enabled to win his
match in six hours and a half!

A propos to the sagacity of the horse—
awkward disclosures will out.   It happened

that a friend of mine had embarked largely
in farming, and, according to the usual free-
masonry of his fraternity, maintained that it
was a losing concern—and that all of his
trade profess all and every year of their lives,
although the crops were fine, that they never
paid him. A horse was the means of discovering that which a Scotch steward either could
not find out, or found it more convenient to
wink at. One evening, just as the workmen
were going home from their daily labour, one
was suddenly called to hold the horse of a
gentleman, who had just arrived. Pat came
forward with a flourish, his hat well on one
side, with an illigant cock, poised upon one
hair, as poor Power loved to appear in the
" Irish Lion," till unluckily the horse, whose
olfactory nerves were not to be deceived, gave
it a gentle push; off rolled the castor, and
out tumbled a shower of oats. " Murder will
out," they say, and now my friend discovered
why his land would not pay; his labourers

being in the daily habit of carrying off hat-loads of corn.

The drivers of the stages and the inhabitants, if halting either for refreshment or for the night, never care to bring their horses cool into the stable, or even to rub them down; but, on the contrary, the perspiration is allowed to freeze upon their coats, which are a mass of hoar-frost by the next morning. They never catch cold, nor are they the worse for it.

It is the custom in this province, and indeed in most of the States, to drive without bearing reins and with snaffle-bits; and so quiet are the horses in harness, that breeching is but rarely used. The drivers in general put the horses into a full gallop, and charge down hill, either when in a waggon or a sleigh— the impetus carrying them some distance up the opposite slope. It would be ridiculous to see horses borne up, champing their bits and tossing the foam from their proud heads, without the corresponding appendage of a fat and jolly-looking coachman, to whose hands the guidance of a perfect London "turn-out" is entrusted; and the amusing author of "the Bubbles" has remarked that, as we bear up our horses to the utmost extent, the Germans go into the opposite extreme, and take great pains to tie the heads of theirs down; but it appears to me, that for work, to say nothing of the comfort of the animal, the Bluenose arrangement is preferable.

Towards the spring, when the ice is expected to break up, the horses are driven with long cords (acting as safety reins), fastened round their necks with a running knot. Should the ice give way, the driver immediately hauls upon the rope until he has, *pro tem.*, strangled the animal. The air, thus confined, inflates him; he floats, and is easily dragged out upon the sound ice, when, the cord being cut, he jumps up, seldom or ever the worse for his immersion.

Every fresh fall of snow obliterates the beaten sleigh-tracks; and, in order to avoid doubtful ice, or air-holes, it is customary to mark out the different crossings over the frozen bays or rivers, by fixing young fir-trees into the ice at intervals : no one can imagine, until caught in a North American snow-storm, what a guide and blessing they are.

Never shall I forget returning to St. John, after a hunting expedition, accompanied by an inhabitant of that place, and being obliged to cross the Grand Bay and part of the Kenebekasis; frozen sheets of water, just above the tide-way; and over which we had sleighed in perfect safety in the morning. The moon shone clear and bright, and we had crossed one half of the Grand Bay; when, all at once, we heard strange sounds, like the clang of hundreds of rifles discharged on all sides in the surrounding forests : it was soon evident whence the noise proceeded — from the effect of the noonday's sun, the ice was

breaking up. It was a route but seldom
ventured over, and was not, for that reason,
marked out with fir-branches. I was confident that, so far, I had kept the right course,
and urged on the horses, who snorted and
showed evident symptoms of terror. Suddenly
the moon became overcast, black clouds began
to gather and darken the heavens; a tremendous storm came on, and the snow beat thick
and fast in our faces. We came to a crack
in the ice at least a yard wide, which extended
across the whole bay; there was no time to
be lost in searching for a narrow place, as the
cracking of the ice became tremendous; so
there was no alternative left but to run the
horses at the chasm, which they cleared in
gallant style, and, by keeping them in full
gallop, in ten minutes we were safe on the
main land. Next day boats were to be seen
upon the water; the ice having totally disappeared.

CHAPTER IV.

OF THE MILICETE AND MICMAC INDIANS.

Lo! the poor Indian, whose untutored mind
Sees God in clouds, or hears him in the wind;
His soul proud Science never taught to stray
Far as the solar walk or milky way;
Yet simple Nature to his hope has given
Behind the cloud-topped hill an humbler heaven;
Some safer world in depth of woods embraced,
Some happier island in the watery waste,
Where slaves once more their native land behold,
No fiends torment, no Christians thirst for gold.
To be, contents his natural desire,
He asks no angel's wing, no seraph's fire;
But thinks, admitted to that equal sky,
His faithful dog shall bear him company.

Origin of the Indians, a Quere—Fossil remains—Mr.
Gesner—Micmacs, or " Salt-water" Indians—Boundary be-
tween them and the Milicete—Render homage to the Iroquois
—Council fire still burns—Their *Totems*—Language—
Papoose—Wigwams — Snow-shoes—Patterns —Old John
and Cockney.

The colour, appearance, and general habits
of the Indians inhabiting North America,
have been often ably described; as often

quite the reverse. And, as the public have lately had the works of Catlin before them, and the Ojibeways as living models, little remains to be said. It would be quite absurd in this slight sketch of the Indians inhabiting New Brunswick to recapitulate the many conflicting opinions, or to enter into the arguments *pro* and *con.*—how or by what means the continent of America [1] was peopled originally; whether Behring's Straits ever were or

[1] " In America the same difficulties present themselves in relation to the origin and propagation of races as in the old world. The most recent inquiries authorized the distinction of two families inhabiting America; first, a race called Toltuan, belonging originally to Mexico and Peru, which from the shapes of the skulls found in the graves and the accompanying relics, give evidence of greater civilization than belongs to the present natives; and, secondly, a people which, extending over the greater portion of the vast continent, embraces all the barbarous nations of the new world, excepting the Polar tribes, or Mongolian Americans, which are presumed to be straggling parties from Asia, such as the Esquimaux, Greenlanders, and Fins.

"In the native American, there is no trace of the frizzled locks of the Polynesian, or the woolly texture on the head of the Negro. The hair is long, lank, and black; the beard is deficient; the cheek-bones are large and prominent; the

were not at any former period dry land, or
whether rocks or islands existed in these
straits; or by what means (if it even were so)
men were ferried over from Asia to people
the continent of America. All this I must
leave to the fertile imaginations of such men
as will try to convince the world that Greenland once formed a part of North America;
that the Esquimaux understand the language
of the natives of that country; and that the
birds and beasts (however much they may
have degenerated by the migration) originally
came from the old world. I have nothing
further to adduce, for my part, than that,
unless the ark was affected by the Gulf Stream
during the forty days that it continued on

lower jaw broad and ponderous, truncated in front; the
teeth vertical and very large; the nose is decidedly arched,
and the nasal cavities of great size. They ought not to be
called the copper-coloured race. The colour is brown, or
of a cinnamon tint. As in the old world, the colour varies,
and the darker shade does not always correspond with the
climate or vicinity to the equator."—*Sir Charles Bell on
"Anatomy of Expression."*

the face of the waters, and that, as it neared the coast of America, a couple of alligators took that opportunity of swimming ashore, that species of reptile must have suffered dreadfully from cold in their " overland passage" either by way of Greenland or Behring's Straits.[1]

Apropos of antediluvian theories, Mr. Gesner has discovered the bones of a large fossil elephant, which had been originally mistaken for wood, and sold in the market of St. John as such. These remains are in his possession, and he has obtained such information as may probably lead to the discovery of the skeletons of other gigantic animals which have long since ceased to exist

---

[1] While permitting myself to speak lightly of the con-flicting opinions of those gentlemen, who each arrange creation to suit their particular theories, I am far from meaning to jest on the sublime descriptions of Genesis. I believe that it has been proved by ship-builders that the dimensions of this wonderful ark are the most perfect that could have been thought of. There cannot be a more striking instance of that divine wisdom "which ordereth all things well."

on the earth. Mr. Gesner is descended from the celebrated Conrad Gesner, who first distinguished the genera of plants from a comparison with their flowers, seed, and fruit. He was employed in making a geological survey of the province, during which time he managed to collect a capital museum of its natural productions, which he sold to the Mechanics' Institute of the city of St. John for £600.

There are in New Brunswick two tribes of Indians, differing most widely from each other in their language, customs, implements, and habits of life; and this striking difference in almost every particular, between two people inhabiting the same country, and evidently sprung from the same common stock, constitutes not the least remarkable point of interest among the many which attach to this singular race.

First in order, not only as the most numerous, but as possessing both moral and physical superiority over the others, are the Micmacs, a tall and powerful race of men, who frequent the north-eastern shores of the province, bordering on the great Gulf of St. Lawrence; and who form part of an Indian nation which extends over Nova Scotia, Cape Breton, Newfoundland, Prince Edward's Island, and Gaspe. The less numerous and inferior body are the Milicete, who frequent the St. John and its tributary waters.

The Micmacs are strongly attached to the sea-side, near which they are generally found; and, from this circumstance, the Milicete commonly call them " the salt water Indians." Their hunting grounds, over which they range uncontrolled, and of which they are supposed to have the sole possession, embrace the whole north-eastern coast of New Brunswick from Baie Verte to the Baie des Chaleurs, and thence extending back to the head-waters of all the streams on that coast, which flow into the Gulf.

The hunting country of the Milicete comprises all the extensive territory watered by the St. John and its numerous tributaries, whether flowing from the eastward or the westward. The boundary between the Micmac and Milicete hunting countries is such a line as will separate the waters flowing eastwardly into the Gulf of St. Lawrence, from those which flow westwardly into the river St. John. The westward boundary of the Milicete hunting country is a line which will separate the waters flowing eastwardly into the St. John from those which flow westwardly into the Penobscot river, in the State of Maine; at the sources of the eastern tributaries of the river, the hunting country of the Penobscot tribe commences.

This last mentioned tribe reside within the limits of the United States, yet they speak the Milicete language, and render homage to the chief of the Milicetes in New Brunswick, whom they regard as their head and leader.

The whole number of Milicetes at present in New Brnnswick is a little short of five hundred ; the number of the Micmacs somewhat exceeds one thousand. The village of the Milicetes is situated on the right bank of the St. John, about ten miles above Fredericton, and on the same side of the river. In the village there is every kind of habitation, from the slight birch-bark wigwam up to the comfortable two-story dwelling-house, owned by an Indian, who, by superior industry and intelligence, has attained a situation above his fellows.

The Milicete language is a dialect of the Huron, the language of the Iroquois, of which once powerful confederacy they formed a branch tribe. The council fire of the Iroquois is yet kept burning at Caughnawaga, an Indian village, on the south side of the St. Lawrence, a few miles above Montreal, where the great chief of the nation resides. A deputation of the chiefs and principal men of the Milicetes proceed every third year to Caughnawaga to report the state of affairs, and take part in the grand council of the nation which is there held.

Those acquainted with Indian history will remember that the Iroquois nation was formed by the celebrated confederacy of the Six Nations, who received the designation of Iroquois from the French, but were called Mingoes by the English. They present the only example of intimate union recorded in the history of the Aborigines, and were by far the most powerful body of Indians upon the continent of America. They consisted originally of five nations, namely, the Mo-hawks, the Onondagoes, the Senecas, the Oneidas, and the Cayugas. About 1717, the Tuscaroras joined the confederacy, and formed the sixth nation: since that period, they have been sometimes known as the Five Nations, but more frequently as the Six Nations. These several nations were subdivided into various tribes and families, and this subdivision was an important part of Indian policy.

The number of these tribes among the various nations was different and perhaps indefinite; they usually extended, however, from five to six, twelve, or fifteen. Each has a distinct appellation derived from some familiar animal, as the bear tribe, the eagle tribe, or the wolf tribe, and the figure of the animal giving name to the tribe became the *totem*, or armorial bearing, of every individual belonging to it. When it became necessary to identify a person in any of their rude drawings, or in later times, when one of them was required to affix his mark to any instrument prepared by the white man, his *totem* was first made, and then any particular characteristic was added which might apply to him individually. The *totem* of the Milicete is the beaver, and a member of the tribe who wished to designate himself would first sketch the figure of the beaver, and then place be-

neath it his own peculiar *totem* or crest, such as
the hawk, or pigeon, the minx, eel, or salmon.

Before the arrival of Europeans in America,
the office of giving names was deputed to the
wise and aged Indians, who had the best
knowledge of the ancient names of their
forefathers, and were most capable of invent-
ing new ones. At that period, such names
as " the sloping sky "—" the pleasant flowing
stream "—" the sparkling light "—" the roaring thunder "—" the leaping panther "—" the
cloud that rolls beyond "— " the noon-day sun"
—were in common use; but their present de-
signations have been acquired very differently.

The Indians of New Brunswick were first
converted to Christianity, and taught the prin-
ciples of the Catholic faith to which they
religiously adhere, by the Jesuit missionaries,
a class of men of whom it must be admitted
that, whatever may have been their sins in the
old world, they have in the new been known
chiefly as the friends, protectors, and civilizers

of a race, forsaken or trampled upon by nearly all besides. When they baptized their converts, they conferred upon them names selected from the calendar of saints; and these names, with those borne by the descendants of French officers, or the early French settlers who intermarried with the Indians, now form nearly the whole of the appellations borne by the Milicetes and Micmacs. In making up the enumeration of these people, Mr. Perley found the names of St. Jerome, St. Chrysostom, St. Boniface, St. Hilaire, St. Geoffroy, St. Augustin, St. Antoine, St. Gregoire, St. Remigius, St. Athanase, and St. Denys, occurring very frequently, while among the women he found quite as common Ste. Angelique, Ste. Pelagie, Ste. Genevieve, Ste. Anastasie, Ste. Monica, Ste. Veronica, and the like.

Many families bear the names of those from whom they have descended among the French; and among the Micmacs, the *St. Juliens*, the *De Pommevilles*, the *De Bois*, the *Des*

F 5

Dames, the *La Roques,* and the *La Bognes,*
are all very numerous. One tall, handsome,
sub-chief, who resides at the Milicete village,
is the descendant of a French officer of en-
gineers, and bears the name of his proge-
nitor, *Vassal la Conte;* and at the same
village, a very pretty young squaw, an orphan,
bears the romantic name of *Cecile le Belmont.*

With their names the Indians of the province acquired much of the dress of the early
settlers, who were principally Basques, Bre-
tons, and Normans; and the picturesque
Basque dress is much in vogue with the
Micmac squaws to the present hour.

The language of the Micmacs is a dialect
of the Algonquin, of which powerful nation
they once formed a large and influential portion. The Algonquin nation formerly num-
bered twenty-two different tribes—the Micmacs, Elchemins, Abenakis, Tokokis, Pas-
tuckets, Pokanokets, Narragansetts, Regnoils,
Mohegans, Lenni-Lenapes, Cor*men,* (as the
Delawares styled themselves), Nanticokes,

Powhatans, Shawnees, Miamis, Illinois, Chip-
pewas, (latterly called Ojibbeway), Ottawas,
Menomonies, Lacs, Foxes, and Kickahoos,
which were again subdivided into more than
a hundred tribes.

The Lord's Prayer, in the Milicete language,
is as follows :—

" Me-tox-sen' a spum-keek ay-e-en sa-ga-mow-ee tel-
mox-se'en tel-e-wee-so-teek. Cheep-tooke wee-chey-u-leek
spum-keektaun e-too-chee-sauk-too-leek spum-a-kay-e'en.
Too-eep-nauk-na-meen kes-e-kees-skah-keel wek-a-yeu-
leek el-me-kees-kaak keel-mets-min a-woo-lee. Ma-hate-
moo-in ka-te a-le-wa-nay-ool-te'ek el-mas we-chee-a-keel
me-koke-may-keel ne-ma-hate-hum-too-moo-in.

In the Micmac language, the Lord's Prayer,
as corrected by the Richibucto Indians from
the version printed at Quebec in 1817, reads
thus : —

" Noorch enen waa-soke a-bin, chip-took, tal-wee-sin
me-ga-day-de-mak. Waa-soke tee-lee-daa-nen chip-took
igga-nam-win oo-la nee-moo-lek naa-de-la-tay-se-nen.
Naa-tel waa-soke ai-keek chip-took ta-lee-ska-doo-lek ma-
ga-mi-guek ay-e-mek. Tel-la-moo koo-be-na-gal es-me-
a-gul opch nega-atch kees-kook ig-ga-nam-win nee-loo-nen.
Ta-lee a-bik-chik-ta-kaa-chik wa-gai-nee-na-met-nik elk-
keel nees-kaam a-bik-chik-too-in el-wa-wool-ti-jeck. Mel-
kee-nin maach win-chee-gul mook-ta-gaa-lin kees-e-na-
waam-kil win-che-gul ko-qui-ak too-ack-too-in.

It is said that in all the vast extent of Canada and the United States there are but three radical or mother tongues—the Sioux, the Algonquin, and the Huron. The Sioux is rather a hissing than an articulation of sounds. The Huron language has great dignity, pathos, and elevation; and the ancient missionaries did not scruple to compare it with the finest languages known. The Algonquin, however, they say, excels the Huron in smoothness and elegance; and, so far as Mr. Perley was able to judge from the Micmac dialect, it far excels the Huron in power, comprehensiveness, and lofty imagery. Both languages, it may be remarked, have a dual number, and in other respects resemble the Greek. All the changes of mood, person, tense, and number are formed by change of terminals. Upwards of two thousand terminals are made on one radix in the Micmac language. It is, therefore, difficult to speak it in all its purity with correctness; yet enough of it may be learnt in a few weeks by a person acquainted with the French, English, and Latin, to converse in it sufficiently well for all ordinary purposes.

The females, when young, are often exceedingly handsome; and that prominency so observable in the cheek-bones of the men is among the women but faintly marked. Their noses are, in general, aquiline, and finely shaped, and their eyes possess a peculiar, soft, and languid expression; the teeth are fine, white, and even; and their magnificent long black hair is carefully parted down the centre, and plaited behind in two long tails, through which is generally threaded some bright-coloured ribbon. I have often seen their plaits reach nearly to the ground. Their figures in early life are fine, with hands and feet peculiarly small; but their gait is ungraceful, as they turn in their feet, and shuffle along with a lateral jerk of the whole body at every step.

Although very handsome women are to be met with among them, they are by no means to be taken as a type of the tribe. They are, in general, plain-looking, and many are frightful. Indeed, all soon lose every trace of good looks, owing to the hardships which they endure, in addition to child-bearing and exposure to all sorts of weather, and that too in a climate so variable as theirs.

No where, with the exception of the unfortunate female peasants of Bavaria, have I seen the weaker sex so degraded. The squaws carry the papoose, and often very heavy burdens; make the greater part of the canoe, and, when completed, have to assist in propelling it; in short, they do all the drudgery: it is, therefore, not to be wondered at that they should become bloated, unwieldy, and prematurely old. I do not recollect to have ever seen a good-looking middle-aged woman among them.

The manners of both sexes are never vulgar,

because they are always naturally courteous.
When they appear in full dress, the squaws
wear a conical-shaped cap or head-dress of
blue or scarlet cloth, embroidered with white
beads, and edged with ribbons; a long frock,
reaching a little below the knees, with scarlet
or blue cloth leggings; in finishing them the
seams are not turned in, but, on the contrary,
the wider they can contrive to have the surplus
cloth on the outside, the more it can be
bedizened with ribbons, beads, and wampum.
Their mocassins, made from moose leather,
are beautifully embroidered with beads. The
Milicete tribes use beads instead of the hair
of the moose, or porcupine quills are employed
for this purpose by most of the tribes in
Upper and Lower Canada, and in the far West.
The front of their dress is fastened with a
number of circular silver buckles, the largest
being placed at the top, and so diminishing
as they descend; but they are more ornamental than useful. These constitute their

trinkets, which they always carry about upon
their persons; and, as cloth is to them expensive, the men generally appropriate that
to their own use; and the poor squaws are
to be most commonly seen in old chintzes and
Manchester cottons: and, with a blanket,
which serves in the severity of the winter as
a cloak by day, and as a bed at night, this
completes the toilette and wardrobe of a
squaw of the Milicete tribe.

To the adorning of the lords of the creation everything is sacrificed among the Indian
tribes without exception. As we say of the
feathered tribe, at least, fine feathers are
supposed by them to make " fine birds."
The male, in the latter case, is always of
more gaudy plumage than his mate; so the
Indian shines resplendent in his decorations
and paint, and his unfortunate squaw hides
" her diminished head." His head-dress,
when in gala costume, is fashioned somewhat
like that described above as worn by the

women, but descends much further down the back, and having two pointed horns of the same material, not unlike horses' ears, on the top of the head: these are embroidered with beads; and the flap which hangs down behind is striped with ribbons of different colours. The coat or hunting-frock does not reach so low as that of the squaw; it is, in general, blue, with scarlet cuffs and collar, richly worked with beads and scarlet cloth let into all the seams as in a lancer's jacket. A broad crimson ribbon generally gives a very pretty finish to the bottom of the coat, and across the back and shoulders is a mass of embroidery.

I have seen some chiefs of the Penobscot tribe with scarlet coats, almost a mass of beads. This is very magnificent; but the white beads, in my opinion, show much better on the blue. From an embroidered shoulder-belt or baldrick is hung the powder-horn; and their knives, tomahawks, and tobacco-pouches or pitchnaugans' skins (entire) upon

which embroidery is attached, are suspended
through their belts of wampum. When the
costume of this tribe is well "got up," it is
almost magnificent.

Papoose is the name applied either to the
infant of the Indian, or the wooden kind of
box or portable cradle in which the unfortunate child is bound. Before the infant is
placed in it, the arms are extended down
the sides and swathed round and round with
cloth or other bandages, until it becomes
like a mummy, in the manner practised by
the Roman mothers at the present day. This
confinement and distortion of the limbs during
infancy are alleged by many to be the cause
of the awkwardness of the Indian's gait when
grown up. The swathing being completed,
the child is placed on its back in the case,
and fastened in it with hoops of hickory or
ash. On the move, the squaws carry the
papoose on their backs ; and, when employed,
hang it up on the nearest branch. The

operation of swathing occupies much time, and the child often remains for long periods thus encased. Nothing but the face appears; and the situation of a papoose thus suspended is anything but enviable, and may easily be discovered by a swarm of mosquitoes and black flies, attracted to the exposed part of the unfortunate brat.

When old enough to be released from this cruel imprisonment, they are suffered to run about naked, and to roll themselves in the mud, until they become sufficiently hardened. " The young idea" soon " learns how to shoot," and to perform astonishingly with the bow and arrow—a practice entirely relinquished by the adult portion of the community, since the Birmingham catch-penny pieces, the vilest of guns, have been introduced into America —though with these they contrive to direct a ball at one hundred yards with the precision of one fired from the best rifle turned out of Moore's or Lancaster's shops.

Every Indian tribe has its peculiar form and pattern for every thing they make and wear— their canoes, wigwams, or snow-shoes; their embroidery on birch-bark, cloth, or leather; in moose hair, wampum, or porcupine quills. The Indian instantly knows, by its fashion, to what tribe the slightest ornament or utensil belongs. All the manufactures of the Milicete are more graceful in their forms and proportions than those of any other tribe I ever saw in any part of North America; and many of their patterns, now that fresco painting has come into vogue, would be beautiful for borders to arabesques, or might be copied in worsted work for the modern species of tapestry which occupies so much of the time of ladies at the present day.

Their canoes are made of one entire piece of bark stripped from the canoe birch, (betala papyracea) which attains to the height of seventy feet, and is often three feet in diameter. It is best when obtained in the winter months—

fire is then applied to make the tree peel—
and a " winter bark" canoe is the article of
most value among the Indian's effects. It is
difficult to find a tree sufficiently clean and
free from knots; and the growth of every
canoe birch sapling of any promise is jealously
watched by the Indian. Who can say that
the hatchet has not been dug up, and that
the flame of war may not have been kindled
in the olden time for so trivial a cause as a roll
of birch-bark ?

The gunwales of the canoe are made of fir,
and the ribs and flooring of white cedar, (the
lightest of all the kinds of American timber),
over which the bark is stretched, and the
whole thing is sewed together with the fibrous
roots of the white spruce, about the size
of a quill, which are deprived of the bark,
split, and suppled in water. The seams
are coated and made water-tight with the
gum of the spruce or balsam firs. Their
average weight may be one hundred and

twenty pounds, their length varying from sixteen to twenty-one feet. An Indian thinks
little of carrying one of them on his head;
in addition to, perhaps, a hind-quarter of a
moose deer, or some such weight, on his
back; and will trudge along at a pace that
would soon tire our best mountain sportsmen.

Into one of their canoes can be packed
enormous loads. I have often seen a family,
fifteen or sixteen in number, besides all their
goods and chattels, stowed away in a birch
canoe, about nineteen feet in length; and, when
loaded in this way to the very water's edge,
they will fearlessly hoist an old blanket by
way of a lug-sail, and "carry on," when
a tremendous sea is running. In order to
preserve their canoes during the winter season,
they bury them in snow—a practice which
fully answers the purpose. Nothing can be
more graceful on the water than a Milicete
canoe; at the same time, so frail are they,
that it generally costs the uninitiated several

good duckings, by way of apprenticeship,
before he learns the use of the paddle, or
even to preserve his equilibrium in them.

The economy of the Indian's hut or wigwam
is perfect. A number of poles are fastened
together near their apex, and the lower extremities extended until the required base is
obtained (and they can be likened to nothing
seen in England but the piles of hop-poles in
Kent after the hop harvest is finished); over
this skeleton work are extended sheets of birch
bark sewed together. A sufficient aperture
is left at top to allow the smoke to escape,
and to do duty for a chimney. The entrance
is cut out of the roll of bark; and an old
blanket or piece of cloth is suspended by way
of door. This covering of bark and the
whole building may be taken down and rendered transportable in a few minutes.

When about to make a permanent camp, or
to remain for any length of time in one particular spot, great neatness may be observed

in the interior economy of their wigwams. The floor is covered, for a space extending round the whole circumference, with the ends of the branches of the silver fir, broken short off and placed one over another, slanting towards ths centre. In the midst is the fire, and four laths of fir accurately determine the finish of the divan and the commencement of the kitchen department. In their cuisine they have made but little progress; and a stone trough, or an old frying-pan, is the utmost limit to which their culinary implements extend.

About their wigwams is to be seen the Indian dog—a cross, in which that of the fox evidently predominates—and the sharp-pointed ears, long, slender, black hairs, and bushy tail, denote their origin. The bodies of these dogs are exceedingly long, their legs as remarkably short. They are very small, and so light as to be able to run over the snow when covered with the slightest crust: they have, therefore, a great advantage when in pursuit of large game, which in that case flounders through it. These dogs are very stanch, and, when once put upon the track of a moose or bear, will not leave it until they bring the one to bay, or " tree" the other. In the winter season, they do good service for the Indian, and are harnessed in couples of two, four, and six, to small sledges.

Neither the Micmacs nor the Milicetes disfigure themselves with paint, or by tattooing : probably the custom has worn out, since their adoption of the Christian religion, and from the length of their intercourse with the European settlers. The Micmac nation, owing to the exertions of Mr. Perley, their adopted chief, have all taken the pledge; and, in all probability, by the endeavours of that gentleman, the Milicetes will be induced to follow their example : but at the time of our sojourn in the province, many of the Milicetes were to be seen drunk about the streets of St. John.

It is, nevertheless, a remarkable trait in the Indian character, that, however they may indulge in the vice when in a town, it is a point of honour with them, when engaged to go on an expedition into the woods, not to touch spirits.

I once took an Indian off from St. John in a hurry, to hunt; and, although I knew that he had been in a state of inebriation for three days previous, and the effects of the debauch had not " died in him," yet when, after a tough chase of four hours and a half, on snow-shoes, I offered him my brandy-flask, he shook his head as he replied, " Me no touch dat in woods, never ;" and he persisted in his resolution in spite of my persuasions.

Notwithstanding the long intercourse they have had with Europeans, and so much as they have been thrown into contact with them, they will not adopt European customs; and they have an innate aversion to civilized life. Great exertions have often been made on the

part of different governors to inculcate do-
mestic habits, to induce them to cultivate
the soil, and to build houses. One of the
chiefs, old Louis Bear, if I recollect right,
at the particular request of one of their excel-
lencies, built a stone house of two stories.
When completed, he requested that the
governor would come and see what he had
done. He had built a house, and had laid
out a great deal of money in the construction
of it; but, on a close inspection, it was
discovered that he had built his wigwam
inside.

I have been informed that the Indians of
the Micmac tribe, generally taken into the
woods by the officers of the Halifax garrison,
are an extremely lazy set, very few of them
good hunters; and those that are so give
themselves great airs. The family of the
Glodes, near Annapolis, and the Indians in
that village, are excellent hunters, as are also
old Saccobe, Joe Lola, Louis Polcis, Louis

Bear, and John Sabbattis, of the Milicete nation (should they be still living). They are the most trustworthy and faithful in the woods; and this tribute, in the shape of a recommendation to any one about to follow the chase in the neighbourhood of Annapolis, in Nova Scotia, or from St. John or Fredericton, in New Brunswick, is paid to their honesty and good-will, by one who had every reason to be satisfied with their exemplary conduct.

I never could persuade my faithful pilot of many trips in " the woods," John Sabbattis, to sleep at an inn, when *en route* for distant hunting grounds; nor would he eat under the roof of one, but would steal off and return at the appointed hour. The Indian, when hired for an expedition, must be treated kindly; he is fed and paid commonly at the rate of a dollar a day; and there is nothing that they will not do for you, provided you treat them with common attention. Much insight into wild life is gained by so doing,

much woodcraft lost by a contrary proceeding; and a good sportsman is in general
gifted with sufficient tact to discover this.

Should any one, however, be unsportsman-
like enough to bully the Indian in the woods,
his high sense of honour will cause him to
keep his engagement inviolate ; he will do
his duty by his employer so long as their
agreement lasts. But such is his independence of spirit, that he will never again go
out with that man ; and no sum of money
will induce them so to do.—One anecdote of
John.

An admirer of nature, and a would-be
sportsman, but whose proficiency in the art
had not advanced him beyond or entitled him
to other appellation than that of Cockney,
heard of the magnificent scenery on the
Musquash lakes ; and, being anxious to com-
bine a little amusement with sight-seeing,
engaged John to take him in his canoe,
and fish, *en passant* the magnificent rapids,

still waters, and creeks, which connect this fine chain of lakes. All this his faithful *cicerone* did in Indian fashion. The fellow behaved, however, to John in the woods pretty much as he would have treated a waiter at a coffee-house, and finally d—d John for not cleaning his boots; while John preserved an inflexible silence. The sportsman, however, was so pleased with the scenery of the lakes, that he wanted to go a second time, and applied to John to accompany him; this the Indian flatly refused to do. Our friend stared, and asked him the reason. John very coolly replied, "Me no walk again with you—me always used to walk woods with gentlemen."

CHAPTER V.

NEW BRUNSWICK——OF THE BIRDS AND BEASTS.

> Where beasts with man divided empire claim,
> And the brown Indian marks with murd'rous aim,
> *　　*　　*　　*　　*　　*
> Or seeks the den where snow-tracks mark the way,
> And drags the struggling savage into day.
> GOLDSMITH.

Passenger Pigeons——Wild and Water fowl——Novel way of gunning——Genus Tetrao——Birch and Spruce Partridge——Humming-birds——Wax-bird——Soirée of Owls——Lucifees——Skunk——Wild Cat——Novel mode of catching Wolves——Musk-rat——Porcupine——Hares——Bears and Chimneys——A sound sleeper——The Governor gammoned.

In the months of June and July, the " passenger pigeons," described by Wilson as darkening the sun for days, when on their migratory flights, arrive in New Brunswick. Their favourite resorts are the neglected clearances overgrown with wild raspberries and strawberries, which are their favourite food; also the great mosses and barrens, covered with cranberries and whortleberries, where they are to be found in great quantities, and from amongst which they rise singly or in pairs, are strong on the pinion, and afford excellent sport. They have a long wedge-shaped tail; and, if the ends of it are cut off previously to putting them into a trap, they are so astonished at the moment they attempt to fly, that they go off quite as game as the best blue rocks of " Red House" celebrity.

The woodcock of the New World is much smaller than that of Europe, and, in the plumage, differs materially, inclining more to a fawn colour, particularly on the breast, where the shades of that colour are beautifully delicate. They appear in the spring for a short time, on their migration northward, and on their return are to be found from the middle of August until driven south by the frosts, which set in generally by the end of October. Their haunts are in the alder and

cedar swamps, along the outskirts of the
" Great Bush," and the margins of the clearances, particularly where they have been
suffered to copse.   In Upper Canada and the
United States, they are very partial to
the Indian corn or maize, when planted in
low lands.   They are very quick on the wing,
and when flushed get up with a shrill whistle.
The woodcock of the Western Isles is the
same as that of North America; and I have
heard that there they are to be met with in
great numbers.

What has been said of the habits of the
woodcock applies to those of the American
snipe; but the latter is rather larger, flies
much more heavily, and, in consequence, is
more easily killed than the European snipe.
It is to be found in abundance at Musquash,
on the St. Andrew's road, on the Water-
borough, at Gagetown, Sheffield, in the
islands on the St. John river, on the Gemseg,
and in the Grand Lake meadows.

A high-couraged pointer, particularly of
the Russian breed, is best adapted to find
woodcocks in these woods, when, by fastening
a bell round their necks, you can never be at
a loss to know when they have come to a
point; a practice generally followed on the
Continent and in the Pontine Marshes. There
woodcock-shooting is managed precisely as in
New Brunswick, and the cover is generally
so thick, that the only chance is to shoot the
birds at first sight. Should any of my readers
have pursued this game in the neighbourhood
of Tre Ponti, they may have encountered that
prince of *cacciatori*, Scapellata, who kills
more woodcocks than any man in Italy; but
he is a most provoking dog to follow, for,
amongst other poaching contrivances, he has
a habit of imitating the noise made by a cock
when flushed so completely as to deceive the
sportsman, to cause him perpetually to cock
his gun, and as often to curse the unfeathered
biped from whom it proceeded.

The duck tribe are very numerous, including the wood-duck, harlequin, and blue-winged teal. An Indian will kill from forty to fifty ducks and geese in the day, on the Grand Lake meadows and Musquash marshes: with his watchful habits, his guarded movements, and the colour of his canoe, exactly corresponding with that of the sedge and bulrushes, he is the man of all others to surprise waterfowl.

On one of our visits to the Musquash marshes we saw numbers of the black duck, so called in New Brunswick, but which is more properly "the dusky duck," *(Anas obscurus.)* These birds take the place of the common wild duck and mallard of Europe, and, although I never saw the latter in North America, I believe that they are often to be met with, precisely similar in every respect. The black duck is rather larger, and is of a dark, dusky colour, with wing feathers of a beautiful copper green. The female is like the common wild duck, but with a deeper shade of plumage.

We tried every possible way to get shots at them, by waiting for their " pass" to and from their feeding-grounds at early morn, and at the last glimmering of twilight, by creeping upon them through the rushes, by having them driven, and by silently attempting to drop down upon them in a canoe, all to no purpose—not a duck was bagged ! But that they were to be shot was certain, and we were told of a gentleman farmer, or sort of squireen, who, it was said, contrived to kill numbers. He lived in a log-house on the opposite side of the marsh to our quarters. We determined upon paying him a visit, in order, if possible, to obtain the desired information as to the manner of shooting black ducks.

After some little difficulty, we succeeded in finding his habitation, but the " bird" him-self had flown. We were not doomed, how-

ever, to wait long in suspense, for the report
of his gun at once pointed out his position,
on reaching which we found the black duck
hunter carefully ensconced in a thick tuft of
flaggers, at the edge of a great flooded marsh,
evidently the feeding-ground of the waterfowl
tribes.   Our friend had well chosen his position ; a couple of black ducks lay by his side ;
in his hand he held a book, and across his
knees lay one of those antiquated long guns,
known as " Queen Anne's pieces."   On inter-
rogating him as to *his* method of surprising
the ducks, we received for answer, " Why I
peruses a novel until the ducks come up near
enough, and then I guess I guns 'em."   This
was conclusive; and, without wishing to "take
a leaf out of his book," we left the gentleman
farmer to the perusal of " Peter Simple," and
to the diversion of waiting for a shot.

   The birch partridge, *(tetrao umbellus)* or
ruffed grouse, and the spruce partridge,
(tetrao Canadensis), or dusky grouse, are

beautiful specimens of the genus Tetrao, and are constantly met with in all parts of the forests. They perch upon trees; and, when suddenly disturbed in the Great Bush, will fly up into the nearest tree, when the whole covey or pack become an easy prey to the American sportsman, who begins by shooting the lowest bird first, and so on; otherwise, should he kill one upon the uppermost branches, its fall would disturb all beneath, and they would instantly fly off: however, when come upon suddenly, amongst brushwood or in clearances, they will get up and fly, like red grouse.

The birch partridge is often called " the pheasant" by the Americans, and Wilson describes the stateliness with which they move about, with their broad, fan-like tail spread out; the drumming, as it is usually called, is a singularity of the species. It is performed by the male alone, and is a kind of thumping, or noise, resembling that produced by striking

two full-blown ox-bladders together, but in-
finitely louder; the strokes at first are slow
and distinct, but gradually increase in rapidity,
till they run into each other, resembling the
rumbling sound of very distant thunder, dying
away gradually on the ear. After a few
minutes' pause, this is repeated, and in a calm
day may be heard nearly half a mile off.

" This drumming is most common in spring,
and is the call of the cock to his favourite
female. It is produced in the following
manner:—the bird, standing on an old prostrate log, generally in a retired and sheltered
situation, lowers his wings, erects his expanded
tail, contracts his throat, elevates the two
tufts of feathers on the neck, and inflates his
whole body, something in the manner of the
turkey-cock, strutting and wheeling about with
great stateliness. After a few manœuvres of
this kind, he begins to strike with his stiffened
wings in short and quick strokes, which become more and more rapid until they run into

one another, as has been already described.
This is most common in the morning and
evening, though I have heard them drumming
at all hours of the day. By means of this
signal, the gunner is led to the place of his
retreat; though, to those unacquainted with
the sound, there is a great deception in the
supposed distance, it generally appearing to
be much nearer than it really is."

There is another peculiarity appertaining
to this bird, which I have never seen mentioned by its many describers: it is that of
burying itself under the snow. This was first
pointed out to me, when on a hunting expedition, by Sabbattis's desiring me to prepare for
a shot. After straining my eyes in all directions, I was not a little surprised to see old
John stoop gently down at my feet, and press
the snow with his hand, when, with a whirr,
whirr, a fine birch partridge burst from the
snow, and flew off, shaking a shower from his
pinions. When about to ensconce themselves,

they charge into the snow with all their might, directing their flight so as to be near the surface, the impetus carrying them some way into it, sufficiently far to prevent foxes and lynxes being attracted to the spot; indeed, so small is the orifice in the snow, the particles of which naturally fall over it, that the un-practised eye might pass numbers of these birds thus concealed. The initiated will, how-ever, soon detect a sea-green spot of reflected light in the disturbed snow. Numbers of these birds become an easy prey to the Indian, who, in the early months of their winter hunting, when the snow is so soft that the birds can easily hide in it, however other game may fail, need never go supperless to bed. Lloyd, in his " Northern Field-Sports," men-tions this same peculiarity in the habits of th black cock and capercailzie, during the Scan-dinavian winter.

Among the most pleasing of our summer visitors were the humming-birds (*Trochis*

Colubris) of the red-throated species, the only one known so far north. Their plumage is principally green, with a gold and orange-coloured necklace about the throat, which showed resplendent in the sun as they would sport into our rooms, following its beams, or haunt the mignonette-boxes placed on the window-seats. We were driven to shooting them with sand, as the only means of obtaining possession of them; but the proceeding was devoid of cruelty, as it only stunned the beauties for the moment, and enabled us to secure them alive. They subsist entirely on the juice of flowers, preferring those which are cupped.

The wax, or cedar bird, *(Ampalis Americana)* which is also called "Recollect," is one among the many beautiful of the feathered tribe which pass their summers in New Brunswick. Most of the secondary feathers of the wings are tipped with pieces of a bright vermilion substance, resembling

chips of red sealing-wax; and as this bird
chiefly inhabits the cedar swamps, where he
makes a surprising chattering, Wilson con-
cludes that Nature has armed the feathers in
this astonishing manner, to protect the ends
of them from the wear which would be caused
by its constant fluttering amidst the cedars.[1]

There are owls of every species, from the
great horned, standing nearly three feet high,
to the diminutive little barred. Colden ex-
patiates in his "History of the Six Nations"
on the great superstition of the Indians

---

[1] I quote from old Wilson, having had his admirable
work on American Ornithology by me in North America,
and I invariably found his remarks faithful and correct.
Not so the generality of the numerous writers on this subject, at the present day; many of them compiling from
books, and totally disregarding Nature. Witness the
dressing which one of the fraternity receives from the
intelligent author of "Essays on Natural History." No
modern writer displays such sound good sense, no one can
give such a natural appearance to his preserved birds as
Mr. Waterton. How different from the wretched, wooden-
looking, stuck-up abortions generally to be seen in most
museums!

with regard to those birds, and the terror they have of them, and mentions how much it displeased them to hear any one mimicking their hooting. No such superstition exists among the Milicetes; for I well remember my first essay at "camping out" in the woods. The party consisted of two others, with Sabbattis and old Saccobè. We had passed the day in fly-fishing amidst the deep black pools and cascades, into which the rivers connecting the Musquash Lakes are broken. Grand sport had we had that day, and it was with the highest degree of satisfaction that we stretched ourselves upon the aromatic bed of silver firs, prepared by our faithful Indians.

The night set in gloriously, one of those in the Indian summer to be appreciated only in the woods. The clear moon shone through the lofty pines, and was reflected from the silvery lake, between their taper stems. The crackling of the dry pine logs, and the stream of smoke from the willow-bark and tobacco

in our tomaugans had long sent all the mosquito tribe to the arms of their particular
Morpheus. Every fresh pile of the dry
timber caused a flame which illuminated the
spoils of the chase; here falling upon a large
porcupine, suspended from the branch of a
tree, a black duck, a heap of gold-coloured
char, mottled with blood-red spots; there,
upon our rifles, rods, and implements of destruction; now, on a pair of ragged nether
garments hung up to dry; then on the copper-
coloured and weather-beaten features of the
Indians, as they lay stretched upon the bare
ground on the opposite side of the fire.

Scarcely had the balmy effects of that
delicious, dreamy sort of sleep, known to
those who have lived in the woods, fallen upon
us, when I was awakened by a holloa from the
stentorian lungs of Sabbattis. On shaking
myself and looking about, I discovered an
immense assemblage of the acknowledged
emblems of wisdom gazing at the party with

owls' eyes. They had been collected by the wonderful powers of mimickry inherent in the Indians, who had assembled this *soirée* of owls as much for our amusement as for a sort of introduction to camp-life. Saccobe and John now both set to work in earnest, and great fun it was. Their imitations of the different hootings were so faithful, that it was scarcely possible to say which was the voice of the bird, which that of the Indian. Every fresh arrival joined in chorus until the birds had the best of it, and fairly beat the Redskins. Up we jumped, *en chemise et sans culottes*, and, one seizing a rifle, another a brand of the blazing pine, we put them all to flight. Thus ended my first night "in bush."

The following will be found a good and simple receipt for preserving the skins of birds and animals, and any so prepared will be found to retain their elasticity for any length of time : — white oxide of arsenic, mixed with soft soap, to the consistency of

paste. Alum, burnt in a wood fire till all the
water has bubbled out, and then pulverized,
may be rubbed upon the skins of specimens
for the same purpose, and may do very well
as a makeshift where the former materials cannot be obtained, until the skins can be given
to the preserver. But they do not come out
as pliable or as well as those prepared with
the arsenical soap.

Bears, and lynxes, called lucifees, are the
only animals of prey in New Brunswick;
vermin are very numerous; among these
is a species of polecat, called a skunk, of
which the Indians are in great dread, and
which they hold in utter abhorrence. This
animal is disgusting beyond description; in
appearance the skunk is very pretty—black,
with white, longitudinal stripes. When
attacked, it rolls itself up in a ball like the
porcupine, bedewing its bushy tail with the
most horribly fetid liquor, which is secreted
in a small bag near the rectum, and with this

it liberally besprinkles its assailants. No living thing can stand the odour; and, should this irresistible weapon of defence touch any part of the dress, it must be immediately burned. Men have been known in New Brunswick to have had an encounter with one of these animals, and to have been obliged to strip off every thing, and return to civilized life almost *au naturel*. In passing along a road on a hot day, it is easy to tell if a skunk has crossed it within twenty-four hours; and horses will make a great piece of work should they get a *niff* of one. The Indians, nevertheless, contrive to kill them, cut out the bag containing the fetid fluid, and eat them as a " delicacy."

In New Brunswick there are two species of the lynx, the first named by the French *Loup Cervier*, whence the English corruption, *Lucifee;* the other, the wild cat. The Loup Cervier, when full grown, measures four feet from head to tail, the tail four inches.

It is generally of a light gray, interspersed with minute spots of black : the tips of the ears and tail are jet black, the throat, breast, and belly white. In shape, it is thick and strong, in height about eighteen inches, the fur long, but thick and fine, extending to the feet. It is fierce and powerful, destroys many hares and partridges, and frequently commits depredations among sheep ; has very sharp strong claws, and climbs trees with great facility. It never attacks man, and is generally taken in traps, baited with a piece of mutton or venison. It is very destructive to deer, passing from tree to tree, until it gets directly over its prey, when it pounces from a lofty branch, and rarely fails in fastening upon the deer's back, holding on by teeth and talons, until the victim sinks from pain and exhaustion.

The Wild Cat is about one quarter less in size than the Loup Cervier, has shorter hair on the legs, and a longer tail, without the black tip. In other respects it resembles the Loup Cervier in nature and habits.

Wolves are not indigenous to the province, but have made their appearance in New Brunswick, following the deer, likewise a stranger, which they have driven before them from the eastern States.

A Mr. Andrews, of St. Andrew's, who carries on an extensive "logging" business, contrived very ingeniously to make great slaughter among a pack of wolves. His saw-mills are on the Lepraux River, about twenty miles from St. John. He was at his camp, about ten miles from the mouth of the river, and about one mile from its shore, in the early part of December, with three of his men. About ten o'clock in the evening, the howling of wolves was heard some short distance off, and in a very few minutes, some forty or fifty of them made their appearance, and in a short time the top of the camp was covered with them ;—but, a torch of birch-bark having been lighted up, the whole drove scampered off.

Mr. Andrews at once thought of a plan to capture some of his unwelcome visitors. Himself and men went to work the next morning, and made about fifty or sixty stakes, three and a half feet long, exceedingly sharp, and hardened them by putting the ends in the fire: and, having driven them in the ground about the camp, with the sharp end upwards, about three deep, they prepared torches made of white birch-bark, and, early in the evening, secured themselves in their camp. About the same time as on the former evening, a large number of wolves again made their appearance, and, as before, took possession of the top of the camp,—about fifty in number— looking down at the inmates through the hole in the top of the camp, left for the smoke to escape. Immediately the torches were lighted up, and the drove of wolves

scampered off in all directions, leaping from
the roof of the camp on the sharp stakes;
and in this way fifteen of these ferocious
animals were destroyed. The excessive light
of the torches through the chimney-hole
caused so great a darkness near the ground
that it prevented the wolves from seeing the
stakes, and they consequently leaped upon
them.

The musk-rat is an amphibious animal,
and resembles the beaver in its habits. It
is about fifteen inches in length, its tail
about a foot, and similar to that of a rat.
It is less afraid of man than the beaver, and
is very frequently found in ponds and creeks
in the cultivated parts of the country. In
ponds and low marshes it generally builds
houses, very similar to those of the beaver;
but on the banks of rivers it burrows in the
alluvial soil, and brings forth a large litter of
young. These the Indians take as soon as
they are of sufficient size, in August and

September, by digging. The skins are not of much value then, but the flesh is excellent, and the Milicetes, who are excessively fond of them, devour immense numbers.

In the spring, the musk-rats, or, as they are more generally called, *musquash*, are driven from the usual haunts by the floods of melted snow and ice, and are then obliged to roam about for some weeks. They are shot chiefly in the evenings, while swimming and seeking food, and their skins form an article of commerce. The fur is used by hatters, and a large portion of the *beaver* hats—all those of the second quality—are made of the fur of the musquash, which is substituted for that of the more expensive beaver. The musquash feed chiefly on the roots of the water-lily, and a large species of fresh-water clam, a shell-fish which abounds in all rivers and ponds in New Brunswick.

The mink is of the otter tribe, but smaller, and proverbially black. Its tail is flat and hairy. It subsists in the same manner as the otter, but is more destructive of poultry, which it kills by taking off the head and sucking the blood. The fur is very handsome when in full season; the *pitch naugans*, or fur purses of the Indians, are made of the skin of the mink.

The porcupine is covered with long brown hair, mixed with stiff, hollow spines, about the size of a small wheat straw. These are of a white colour tipped with black, sharp at the end, and are commonly called quills. It dwells in hollow trees, or in cavities under their roots; and feeds on nuts, buds, and the cones of the balsam fir (*abies balsamifera*). Its flesh is palatable and nutritious. The quills are much valued by the Indians, who dye them of various brilliant colours, and use them in ornamenting their mocassins, belts, birch-bark baskets, and boxes.

The Micmac name of the porcupine is "*Madawas*," and hence "*Madawaska*," or

" *the country of the porcupines*," the name by which the territory above the grand falls of the St. John is known, and about which so much has been said, in reference to the Ashburton treaty.

A few beavers are still to be found in the northern or upper part of New Brunswick, although fast yielding to the encroachment of civilization.

There are many racoons in the province, but it is a rather curious fact that none are to be found in the Madawaska country above the great falls.

Hares are very numerous in New Brunswick. Rabbits do not exist; but the hare in these countries is a different animal from the European, inasmuch as it " goes to ground "

Lepus Americanus of Linnæus. Tail short, hind-legs half longer than the body, tips of the ears and tail gray. Inhabits North America, shelters by day under and in the hollows of trees; does not burrow, breeds twice a year, brings five to seven young. Fur gets longer and more silvery farther north; eight inches long: hind-legs longer than common hare; flesh good.

under the roots of trees and into decided
burrows, which is not the case with the latter.
The ears are long, and become perfectly
white during winter. The market at St. John
is plentifully supplied with them during the
winter months, when they are brought in
frozen. Numbers of the spruce partridge
likewise come in frozen at the same time.

Wherever the forest has suffered from fire,
raspberries spring up in quantities; these are
the favourite food of the bear. In winter
bears lie in a torpid state in some hollow tree;
a scathed pine is generally selected, sur-
rounded by a thick undergrowth of birch and
raspberries, which have succeeded the devas-
tation caused by the fire. The greatest care
is taken by Bruin to obliterate all traces of
his abode; but, owing to the searching eye
of the Indian, certain scratches of the animal's claws on the charred surface of the
tree disclose his winter quarters, when an axe
soon prostrates the tree, which, bursting in its

fall, bundles Bruin out, to his great astonishment.

The only opportunity I ever had of shooting a bear was when, lying down to rest upon
a cranberry barren, a huge she-bear came
trotting along with her cub, when, just as I
was in the act of firing at her, the Indian
knocked up the rifle. They will parry any
blow made at them with an axe with the
greatest ease, and, when accompanied by their
young, the Indians generally give them a wide
berth, for, if then wounded, they will rush
upon their assailant.

In the chase of the bear, the Indians prefer
slugs to a single ball, as the latter, unless it
strikes point-blank, will not penetrate the
skull, and, if not killed dead (by being shot
through the brain or heart), they will often
suddenly spring up and show fight. But a
very experienced hand will *hug* a bear, and
choke him, by dexterously seizing him by
the windpipe.

A brother officer and myself purchased a
couple of bear-cubs, so young that they were
obliged to be reared with the greatest care.
A Scheidam bottle was filled with milk and
the muzzle covered with vellum, from which
they contrived to suckle themselves perfectly;
this I mention, having read of the great difficulty of rearing very young bears. For six
weeks they stuck to their bottle, and were the
most innocent and interesting little blue-eyed
rascals, very playful, and would lick any one's
hands like a calf. But as they increased in
stature they took to climbing and malpractices,
until they became an absolute nuisance. They
would climb up any thing from the big drum
to a chimney. One fine day, a review was
ordered, and, as most of the officers' servants
were in the ranks, they took the precaution to
lock their masters' doors. On the parade
being dismissed, one of them, who had locked
his master's door carefully, was not a little
surprised to find a shaving-brush stowed

away in a boot, a powder-horn in a jug, and tooth-brushes in that piece of furniture which " the most absent man in the world" put into his bed, placing himself where it usually stands. This was the servant's account, whether true or not; the chimney was the only way by which they could have entered. Many reports of this sort obliged us to tie up the no longer little Bruins; and, their mischievous practices increasing, they were made over to another regiment when we moved to Upper Canada.

Apropos to the convenience of chimneys to gentlemen of the light-fingered fraternity. A story is told of a regiment quartered in Porto Bello Barracks, (Dublin) which was ordered to muster as strong as possible on the "Fifteen Acres," and, as before stated, all hands were to attend, a trick of the above kind was played by a species of sable bipeds called chimney-sweepers, who got over the barrack wall at some convenient distance from the sentinels, and, by beginning at one end, succeeded in sacking and carrying off a quantity of epaulettes, sashes, and *roba* of that sort generally to be found lying about in officers' quarters.

The thieves who haunt the Dublin barracks are the most inveterate in the world. A flagrant case occurred to an officer whom I relieved on guard at the royal barracks. He had lain down on his bed and fallen asleep, and when he awoke to a sense of his situation, it was not like the hard-goers of the old Irish school, immortalized by Sir Jonah Barrington, to find that his head, after a three nights' debauch, was so firmly fixed in a fresh plaistered wall that it required to be dug out with a pickaxe ; but to discover the loss of both of his epaulets, which had been abstracted by one of a certain class of females haunting the *locale*, who actually cut them off his shoulders whilst enjoying his " beauty sleep."

That my friend was a pretty good sleeper may be inferred from an adventure he had when dining out in the neighbourhood of Durrow. He had gone in a hack-chaise, which, during the time that he was enjoying his claret, was left standing before the hall-door. My friend, who found sundry chasse caffés, or rather "night-caps" of "raspberry poteen," excellent, got quietly out of the room, "whilst the horses were putting-to," and tumbled into the "yellow agony," calling lustily to the boy to drive on. He fell asleep in a moment, and only awoke in the morning to find himself still before the door of his hospitable entertainer, the "putting-to" having existed only in his own imagination. *Mais revenons à nos moutons.*

The flesh of a young bear is excellent; and the paws, in particular, are reckoned a greater *bonne-bouche* than the tongue of the reindeer, the hump of the bison, the tail of the beaver, or mouffle of the moose. So delicious is it, that, on one occasion, the governor of the province, a gourmand and courtier, on his way to the seat of government, dined at the mess at St. John, and ate plentifully of a haunch of bear, smothered in currant-jelly, made most complimentary speeches as to the known reputation of the " *comme-il-faut* mess," begged to know how they contrived to have such capital *mutton*, and wound up by declaring he had never eaten better in his life.

CHAPTER VI.

NEW BRUNSWICK—OF THE DEER, AND WOOD-CRAFT.

——— tum figere damas,
Cum nix alta jacet, glaciem cum flumina trudunt.

Thus nature, like an ancient free upholster,
Did furnish us with bedstead, bed, and bolster;
And the kind skies (for which high Heaven be thanked!)
Allowed us a large covering, and a blanket."

Moose—Cervus Hibernicus, not Antediluvian—Caraboo —Accidents "will happen"—Virginian Deer—Toggery for the Woods—Snow Shoes—"Mal à la raquette" prevented— Hints—Wood-craft—Lose way—Escape being frozen.

New Brunswick was the favourite resort of the moose, but in the early settlement of the province, they were destroyed in thousands, for the sake of their hides and tallow. At present they are rarely to be met with, but are, according to the accounts of the Indians, likely to become numerous again, as they are gradually finding their way back from Canada and Maine, in search of their favourite "moose-wood," so plentiful on the upper St. John.

That the moose deer, or elk, *cervus alces*, at present inhabiting the continents of Northern Europe and America, is a totally different animal in its construction from the so-called fossil moose, found in the bogs of Ireland, has long since been ascertained. Of this the want of the brow-antlers in the moose-deer or elk is of itself sufficient proof. Pennant, in his Arctic Zoology, writes—" I lament that I am not able to discover the animal which owned the vast horns so often found in the bogs of Ireland, so long and so confidently attributed to the moose." He quotes the size of different horns which have been found sometimes " eight feet long, fourteen between tip and tip, *furnished with brow-antlers*, and weighing three hundred pounds; the whole skeleton is frequently found with them."

MOOSE "RUN DOWN."

This deficiency of the brow-antlers alone would at once prove that it is not the same animal : however, I add some very important and curious facts relative to the " *cervus Hibernicus*," as furnished to me by Mr. Glennon, of Suffolk Street, Dublin, whereby it will be clearly seen that they were not antediluvian, and that they bore in their configuration a great similarity to the present fallow-deer—*cervus dama*.

The moose-deer inhabiting North America is the same species as the elk of Europe—the term moose being no other than the name given to that animal by the Algonquin Indians, once the most powerful tribe in North America; "moosu" (the final u is hardly pronounced) being their name for the elk. The French Canadians call it the "Original." The horns of the elk or moose-deer at present inhabiting the continents of Northern Europe and America have no brow-antlers, but a mere continuation of the palm snags, and rarely are found to measure above four feet from tip to tip, in a straight line, whereas those of the fossil moose, so called, *(cervus Hibernicus)*, have been found to measure nearly ten feet across. Mr. Glennon has at present a set of horns that measure in a straight line from tip to tip nine feet six inches, and by the curve sixteen feet six inches, and in a perpendicular line, from the nose to the nearest spike, six feet three inches.

The reindeer, male and female, have horns, and the brow-antlers are fingered, palmated, standing edgeways, and are a continuation of the great palm.

The stag's or red deer's horns are round and not palmated, and have a continued row of brow-antlers on each horn, or to where it is crowned at top, numbering from one to four.

There is therefore no species of the deer tribe at the present time existing, having brow-antlers and palmated horns, but the fallow-deer. Further, the skull or os frontis of the cervus Hibernicus is short by comparison with the great length of the horns, which would give it the exact appearance of the fallow-deer; whereas the present moose-deer or elk has an unusually large, long, and ugly head.

Mr. Glennon has in his possession a skeleton of the cervus Hibernicus, which is nine feet six inches long, seven feet six inches from the coffin bone of the hoof to the top of the bony process of the dorsal vertebræ, and seven feet six inches from the hoof-bones of the hind foot to the top of the pelvis bone. When standing with the head and neck reined up, it would have required eighteen feet head-room. From the contour of the skeleton, it has the appearance of standing square hip to shoulder, like our common fallow-deer, which he declares to be decidedly *the only living type* of that stupendous and noble animal : and, like the fallow-deer, the female was without horns.

Mr. Glennon has further informed me that, together with Mr. Lesly Oglevy, a gentleman

of great research, he has travelled through
the greater part of the counties of Cork,
Kerry, and Waterford, in which there are
scarcely any deposits of calcareous tuffa, which
consist of pulverized limestone, vegetable and
mineral acids, and decomposed vegetable
mould; in these are found the cervus Hibernicus, and not in shell marl, as it is vul-
garly supposed—" as it would take," I quote
his own words, " more fresh and salt water
shells than ever existed from the time of
Noah to the present day, to form such beds
of calcareous tuffa as those contained in Ireland, and in which the remains of the fossil
deer are discovered." And, after stating that
he has discovered that neither the male nor
female had a wagging tail, as he can prove by
several bones attached to different pelvises,
he comes to the most important point of all,
and he goes on to give his reasons for believing
that the cervus Hibernicus, or fossil moose-
deer, so called, is *not* antediluvian.

"I likewise believe that the animal has been slaughtered by man for food long after Noah's time; and, as a proof of the above assertion, I am enabled to discover their remains by landmarks and different vegetables, such as the hippuris, or mares-tail, or German rush, the dwarf willow, and always in the neighbourhood of Danish raths or forts, as they are called. And, further, as another proof of their having been killed by man, I have found in one pit six perfect skeletons of the male, and one head of which I could not find one single bone belonging to the skeleton; and many of the bones of those composing the six had marks of hatchets or choppers upon them; and buried with them in the same hole I found the bones of oxen, horses, pigs, and birds."

The caraboo (the reindeer of Europe) differs in many respects from the rest of the deer tribe. Both male and female have horns, the antlers are of all shapes, those than the female's. The hoof is large, round, and shaped like an ox's, and, from the peculiar formation of the feet, which divide nearly up to the first or fetlock joint, the animal is enabled to gallop over glare ice, clanging his hoofs together with great noise. A New Brunswick lumberer declared to me, that he once drove a caraboo on the Grand Lake, when frozen over (a sheet of water some fifty miles in length), and after an exciting chase on skates, he succeeded in tiring him fairly out, and killing him with his axe.

All other of the deer tribe browse upon leaves, the young shoots of trees, or under cover. The caraboo, on the contrary, love to feed upon the mosses growing on the great barrens or plains, in the spruce fir forests, called caraboo barrens (upon which the large American cranberry grows). In winter, so long as the snow remains soft, they scrape it up with their feet to get at their favourite

mosses ; but, when it is frozen too hard, they
are driven to feed upon the hanging lichens,
and on the stunted firs, struggling to vegetate
on the spongy soil. They find pickings, too,
under the banks and along the edges of the
frozen lakes. Further, Nature has endowed
these animals with such instinct, that, towards
the spring of the year, when the heat of the
noon-day's sun has melted the surface of the
snow in the woods, no power can drive them
into it, where they would sink up to their
bodies and be easily overtaken ; but they will
remain upon the frozen lakes, round and
round which they gallop until they drop dead.
The venison is not so good as that of the moose
or the common deer.

The deer *(cervus Virginianus)* were not
indigenous in the New Brunswick forests, but
have found their way up from the Eastern
States, driven it is said by the wolves. They
are about the size of the red deer of Europe,
are the most graceful of their species, with a
long tail, which when alarmed and in the act

of bounding through the forests, they have
the power of turning over their backs: it
is an object very perceptible in the woods,
from its whiteness, and, when seen in this
position by the hunter, he may receive it as a
warning that it is the last of the animal that
he will see that day. They have been very
numerous in the province of late years; but
their old enemies the wolves have found them
out and are fast thinning them off: they are
seldom to be seen east of the St. John river,
never in Nova Scotia.

The months of March and April are the
best to hunt the caraboo. After a fresh fall
of snow, I used to sleigh as far as Mather's (a
tavern so named after its landlord, an old
soldier, and a jolly dog), and there, leaving
my horses, set off on snow-shoes, accompanied
by an Indian, in a south-westerly direction,
some ten or twelve miles, to the Bald Mountain,[1] the neighbourhood of which is the
favourite haunt of caraboo.

[1] The Bald Mountain, so called from a large cap of white

The Indians, so eager in the chase, are dis-
gusted beyond measure at any failure in
killing or at missing a shot on the part of the
white man. With ever so ordinary a gun,
they contrive to shoot true with a single ball.
They have the greatest possible respect for a
good shot; and I had established my reputation among them, as such, by the merest accident. I was in old Saccobè's canoe — his
favourite canoe the "Waptook" (wild goose),
and was accompanying Mr. Gesner and a
large party, who were ascending the Salmon
river, at the head of the Grand Lake, upon
a geological survey. Six or seven canoes
were paddled in line up the beautiful river,

granite on its summit, is the great feature of that part of the
country, and well repays the trouble of climbing to the top,
by the magnificent view (unlike any thing in Europe) obtained over the great forest, interspersed with countless
frozen lakes. To the north, the view extends over the line
of the Oromuc as far as Fredericton and the St. John's
river; to the eastward, over the Bay of Fundy, and the coast
of Nova Scotia; and to the south lies Passamaquoddy Bay,
studded with thousands of islands—most especially striking
is the stillness which reigns over the whole.

when Saccobè pointed out a small bird of
the dotterel tribe, perched upon the top of a
fantastically-shaped rock of granite, in the
midst of the stream, about eighty yards off.
I took up my rifle, and knocked the bird over.
A simultaneous shout from all the Indians
reverberated through the woods, echoing far
and near; and I lay down that night on my
" spruce bed," an established " crack shot "
amongst the Milicetes; but I repeat that it
was a lucky shot, and the probability is that I
should not have succeeded again in twenty
times.

However, my reputation suffered a severe
reverse the following winter when in company
with Sabbattis. I had followed the trail of
nine caraboo for two days. By the state of
the frozen tracks, the Indian can tell to a few
minutes how far the game is ahead: John at
last declared we were close to them. A frozen
lake lay below us. We walked a great circle
to ascertain whether they had left it. After

a long fag, and just as we had completed the
circle, we debouched upon a narrow point,
running into the lake, when we saw them all,
following in Indian file, and browsing along the
banks. Unperceived, we slipped off our snow-
shoes, and raced to the other side of the point;
and, the wind being favourable, lay down
in the hopes of their feeding our way. I had
a German rifle, one barrel smooth, but both
loaded with ball : the deer came so close that
I fancied by rolling down a second ball I
should have a better chance of killing more
than one. Fired—missed—the balls flew too
high; one had slightly rased the skin, but did
no further damage; the rifled barrel missed
fire, snow having got into the nipple. John was
frantic, and, being a Catholic, invoked all the
saints in his calendar—a very limited one.
The deer, which immediately started off on
my firing, were now as suddenly stopped by
John's shouting and roaring, and formed up
in a half circle in front of us. John thun-

dered out " Load !" I shook in the powder
—the ramrod stuck in the greased rag, and
no power could move it, at least, not his ; he
tore at it with his teeth, and blasphemed to a
fearful average. I put on a cap and fired off
ramrod and all ; one went off limping and we in
chase ; but the traces and blood in the track
became fainter ; he was evidently gaining
strength, so we gave in, and abandoned the
chase.

This is mentioned also as an instance of
the great fag and disappointment which frequently occurs to the caraboo hunter. It is
useless to pursue them, for, when once
alarmed, if not wounded, they will gallop
right ahead for four and twenty hours :—
fresh tracks must be searched for, or the
hunter may as well leave that district.

The operation of walking upon snow-shoes
is a knack in which those only succeed who
have a liking for it. The soldiers of the regiment were drilled upon them previously to

their march over "the Portage" to Quebec,
in 1837; and while some picked up the
method at once, others floundered about, and
only accomplished it with the greatest fatigue.
These snow-shoes, upwards of four feet in
length, are of an oval shape; the light bow
or framework is made of tough ash, in the
manner of a racket; and a fine network of
the sinews of the caraboo is threaded across
it. They are attached to the feet by thick
thongs made from the skin of the same animal; these are crossed over the toes; by
which the snow-shoes are dragged or rather
jerked forward. There is so much spring in
them when well constructed, that, when the
snow is in good order, and the walker in good
practice, thirty miles a day may be accomplished with comparative ease. It is necessary to wear three or four pair of thick
woollen socks under the mocassins to prevent
the toes from being lacerated;—the Indians
substitute a piece of flannel doubled, and

which, perhaps, is preferable.   On coming to
a descent when on snow-shoes, by sitting
down upon them, and holding the heels fast
to guide them, one slides down in the manner
of a *montagne Russe.*

The produce of the chase is dragged out
of the woods upon thin boards, eight or nine
feet in length, called *tabaugans,* turned up
at one end to prevent their hitching in the
snow.   The venison is packed upon them,
and covered over with a blanket.   With the
exception of going up hill, the labour of
hauling them is not great, as they slide over
the snow : when descending, they are slid in
front, and restrained by the tow-line.

A dress made of white blanket, which from
its texture throws off the snow, and from its
colour is not observable in the woods, is best
suited for winter hunting.   The coat should
be made as a hunting shirt, or double-breasted.
The waist is confined by a broad leather belt,
from which hangs a scabbard to hold the

hunting-knife, and through it is thrust a small axe or tomahawk. To these should be added a tinder-box, a pocket compass, and a *pocket pistol*, containing a small quantity of brandy for the use of self, to be used *medicinally*, as the teetotallers have it; for, as I have said, an Indian, however drunk he will get in the towns, makes it a point of honour never to touch spirits when in the woods : his duty is to carry biscuits, salt pork, a kettle, and a frying-pan, rolled up in a blanket, which serves as a cover at night.

A certain degree of tact is required in selecting the spot best adapted for camping for the night, and it is necessary to begin the operation two hours at least before sundown. Firewood, water, and shelter, are indispensably necessary. Numbers of white pine are to be found of an enormous growth, which, having died from old age, stand bleached and scathed among the living mass. One of these, when cut down, will, as it falls, splinter into a thousand pieces. The largest slabs serve to cover in the back of the camp, and the remainder are piled close to the fire—this burns like tinder. A live tree must likewise be cut and hewn into lengths for back logs, which, from being green, burn but slowly.

The fire made, the snow is shovelled out with the snow-shoes to the required size, until the frozen earth is quite cleared, over which is then laid a thick covering of the ends of the branches of the silver fir, broken off short by the hand, and layer placed over layer in the manner of a tile roof, slanting towards the fire. Two upright forked sticks are driven into the ground, across which is laid a long pole, and against it, at an angle, the pine planks (when a pine is not to be had, then birch-bark or fir branches are used), and the snow which was shovelled out is packed round the outside to make all airtight. The camp completed, the snow-shoes are stuck upright in the snow, at a sufficiently moderate distance to dry them gradually ; the socks, &c., are hung upon the cross beam overhead, and the venison and tabaugans so placed that wolves or lynxes may not take a fancy to them.

Thus encompassed by a wall of snow some three feet high, and with one's feet towards a roaring fire, it is sufficiently snug; but towards morning, when the fire burns low, although your feet may be enjoying the luxury of an even temperature, your head and shoulders recline in that of some twenty or thirty degrees below the freezing point. When awakened, therefore, at intervals by the intensity of the cold, an armful of the dry pine wood comes into play. An Indian hates to be roused to perform this office. He either does not feel the cold, or is too idle to stir, and I always found that they disliked it more than being asked to carry great weights for a whole day, or other severe fag ; in fact, it is

the only sort of trouble they object to. I
therefore always made up the fire myself,
particularly as the exertion of shaking them
was even greater than the trouble of heaping
on the wood.

Any one who has encamped in Indian
fashion knows the amusement of barking birch
by way of pastime.   It peels beautifully, layer
after layer—a decided improvement upon the
Yankee fashion of " whittling "—and clean
plates are not required when it is to be had.
The Indians make the greatest use of it.   It
covers-in their wigwams, is sewed together
for that purpose, and, when they move, is
rolled up.   Their canoes, boxes, and in short
all their utensils, are made of it.   Birch-bark
torches light instantly, burn brilliantly, and
emit the most delicious aromatic fragrance.

After a good supper, we lit our pipes, and,
the fatigues of the chase being talked over
and forgotten, I used to listen to old John's
interesting accounts of his hunting expedi-

tions, his manner of finding game, the power of keeping his course through the woods, his adventures, escapes, and endless tales of the forest.

When in the woods, the Indians never call to each other, as a *whistle* does not disturb game so much. It is to be recollected, whenever an halloo is required, that the voice will echo in the opposite direction to the mouth from which the shout proceeds; so, should the person turn round at the same time, the sound will appear to come from all parts of the wood. This, therefore, causes great perplexity. All kinds of deer will stop short when hallooed at sharply, even when alarmed and galloping ever so fast through the forest; they imagine themselves to be running into danger, and therefore halt for an instant only; long enough to glance round; that is the moment when the Indian fires.

The bark of the white willow, when dried, is a good substitute for tobacco, and when mixed with it is very agreeable, and modifies the strong oily taste.

With the Labrador tea *(ledum latifolium)*, and a small evergreen leaf, called wintergreen *(gaulthæria procumbeus)* the Indians make bitter but refreshing beverages. The way they procure sugar is, by tapping the rock or sugar maple when the sap is running up; the tree bleeds profusely, and the stuff, when boiled, makes excellent sugar. The wood is very tough, and from it are made canoe paddles, the jaws of the salmon spears, &c. When in an unhealthy state, enormous excrescences grow from this tree; from these the beautiful bird's-eye maple is cut for veneering; it is not, as is generally supposed, a distinct species.

South-westerly winds prevail towards the autumn; consequently, the young shoots, and, in fact, the whole of the tops of the pines, incline to the north-east. The trees, when blown down at this season, also lie in the same direction; and, in thick weather, the Indian mainly depends upon these signs for keeping his course; but for the same purpose he examines the bark of the hard wood, and discovers by its roughness on what side the tree is exposed to the north-east gales and snow-storms.

To strike a light, iron and stone are indispensably necessary; an excrescence growing upon the black birch makes excellent tinder; this, ignited, is put into a heap of dried splinters, almost powder, obtained from the interior of the pine; all is then placed in a piece of birch-bark, and whirled round until the action of the air causes it to blaze.

But how well versed soever in woodcraft, let no one ever go into the woods without an accurate knowledge of the locale of the country, the general course of the rivers, the situation of lakes, and the direction of any roads which may be in the district, for he can never know, in the eagerness of the chase, what accident may separate him from his guide or party; above all, let him never be without an axe, a compass, and the means of making a fire.

Never shall I forget having parted, on one occasion, from my guide, near the Bald Mountain, confident in the power of finding my way out, some eight or ten miles to the Nerepis road. We had had a hard day's work; the effect of the noonday sun upon the snow had been great; the crust had completely disappeared, and my snow-shoes sunk deep at every step; I became fagged, could not recollect, or was not satisfied with the appearance of the timber and frozen streams passed; became more and more confused, dead beat, and fell often. The horror of being frozen to death came upon me; I was without the means of striking a light or making a fire: I had heard that the only thing to be done in such an emergency was to beat the snow down into a circle, and run

round it all night—a most consolatory pro-
spect for a man dead-beat. Night was coming
on fast; I floundered on and on, when, just
as I was about to give in, I stepped into the
sleigh-track, which told me I had struck the
Nerepis road. The sort of ecstacy in which
I slipped off my snow-shoes is indescribable;
and so confused had I become, that I ran
along the road for nearly half a mile in the
opposite direction to Mather's before I found
out my mistake.

CHAPTER VII.

NEW BRUNSWICK—OF THE FISH AND FISHING.

> When artful flies the angler would prepare,
> This task of all deserves his utmost care ;
> Nor verse nor prose can ever teach him well
> What masters only know, and practice tell.

Salmon spearing—Sturgeon and Molly Greenbaize — Shad
—Gaspereaux—Bass—Flies—The Curry-Curry, gaudy and
large, the best for North American waters—Matty Blake
and the " Yolly Buff"—Receipts for dying—Mosquito mixture.

The rivers of New Brunswick are frequented by a great variety of fish, which
ascend them annually to spawn. The principal of these are the salmon, sturgeon, bass,
shad, gaspereau, smelts, and some others
of less importance. The rivers also abound
with a great variety of fish, which are
constantly found in these waters, and never

descend to the sea. These are the trout,
perch, (red and white) eels, cusk, carp, wach,
dace, gudgeon, bleak, gizzard-fish, and an
infinite variety of others, some of which have
not even a name, and are yet undescribed by
any professor of natural history.

When the salmon make their appearance
in the Nashwak, fleets of canoes, each containing a couple of Indians, leave Fredericton
to spear them by torch-light. The fish,
checked by the falls, are collected in great
numbers in the pools below. Nothing can be
more exciting than this scene—the canoes
hurled about in all directions by the foaming
tide, the skill displayed by the Indians in
forcing them up the rapids, and fending them
off the rocks, or allowing them to plunge
head-foremost down stream, when they suddenly bring them to, and transfix their fish.
The eagerness of the chase, the contrast of
the flaming torches with the black masses of
the woods, and the fine attitudes of the men,

dashing at the salmon with their long spears, form a wild and most animating picture. The spear, which is most destructive, is very simple in its construction, and does not lacerate or spoil the fish. A spike of iron is fastened between two jaws made of rock maple, into the end of a long light fir pole. When the fish is stuck, the jaws open far enough to allow the spike to pierce and break the vertebræ of the spine, and, closing round the fish at the same time, hold it fast.

The sturgeon of the New Brunswick waters are large, frequently eight feet in length, and sometimes twelve. They are a coarse fish, not at all esteemed, are seldom caught or molested, and therefore abound. When running up stream, they leap out of the water to a great height. A good story is told of an old squaw: whilst paddling down the river, one of these fish jumped on board her canoe, with such impetus, that it must have gone clean through the bottom, had not Molly

SALMON-SPEARING BY TORCHLIGHT.

Greenbaize, quick as lightning, seized it by
the tail before the head and shoulders of the
fish had got well through; and, its progress
thus arrested, it did the duty of a plug, until
she contrived to work her canoe ashore.

The trout-fishing is excellent, and nowhere
to be surpassed; except, perhaps, in Labrador.
No sooner does the ice break up, than
myriads of flies appear upon the water, and
the trout come upon them at once. The
Indians, not being disciples of Izaak Walton,
know no other means of fishing for them
than by cutting a hole in the ice, when the
fish instantly come to the aperture, and will
take almost any kind of bait; they, however,
do not consider them worth the trouble of
fishing for, and only resort to the piscatorial
art when in actual want, on a hunting expedition, or when other game fails. In the
Redhead River, some few miles from St.
John, are to be caught the most delicious
trout: it is a back-water frem the sea, and is

occasionally affected by it at very high spring
tides, a circumstance which, no doubt, has its
influence on the flavour of the fish.   In the
Lough Lomond lakes, also in the chain of
lakes beyond the Bald Mountain, having their
outlet in the Musquash marshes, and in the
rivers connecting these lakes, the fly-fishing
is excellent.

The shad, "*clupea alosa*," is a valuable
fish, and bears so much resemblance in its
general conformation to the herring, as to
be called by the New England fishermen "the
mother of herring."   This fish is from three
to seven pounds weight; has a sloping head,
body tapering towards the tail, teeth small
and sharp, dorsal fin nearly in the centre, ab-
domen sharp and serrated, tail forked, back a
dusky blue.

The gaspereau, "*clupea vermalis*," holds
a middle place between the shad and herring, having the general characteristics of
both   and   similar   habits.   Vast quantities

are pickled aud smoked both for home and foreign consumption. They begin to ascend the rivers in April, and continue ascending until July. They are taken in quantities, with large landing-nets, in the pools below the rapids, in the eddies, and in the cavities of the rocks.

Bass is a Dutch name for a species of perch known as the rock bass, or striped bass, (*perca labrax.*) On the sides are parallel lines, like narrow ribbons, eight in number, whence the name of striped bass. Next to mackerel, this is the handsomest of the native fishes of New Brunswick.

Striped bass are sea fish, but principally subsist near the mouths of rivers, which they ascend as high as they can conveniently go. On the approach of winter, instead of striking out into the deep water of the open ocean, the bass finds a residence in ponds, coves, rivers, and quiet arms of the sea, where, undisturbed and comfortable, it remains till the following spring. The bass weighs from three to forty pounds. The largest are taken during the winter, by night-lines, on the Gemsey, and the deep, still streams called the " thoroughfares," which connect the grand lake with its tributary lakes. Such great destruction of bass has taken place on the northern rivers of New Brunswick, particularly the Richibucto, by cutting holes in the ice, and lifting the fish out with dip-nets in very severe weather, when the bass were lying in a torpid state, that special enactments have been made to prevent this waste of the finny tribe.

In sharp tide-ways, during the summer, they are readily caught with trolling tackle and a small fish as a bait : with a salmon rod they afford fine sport.

I would fain say something of the flies best suited to the New Brunswick waters ; but on this subject no two fishermen ever agree : it is proverbial that doctors differ, that ladies

differ, that statesmen differ — but no people
so much as fishermen in the momentous affair
of the choice of flies. It is well known to
those whose experience is worth consulting,
that the fly which will kill well in one water
would not be looked at by the fish in another;
and, moreover, trout are so capricious, that
the fly at which they will rise freely for one
hour in the day, the next they will not even
look at; or, if they do, it is to rise false and
endeavour to drown it by slapping at it with
their tails; and thus it happens that many
fish are caught by being " hooked foul," as
the fishermen term it.

It may be given as a general rule, however,
that as the insects of the new world are both
larger and brighter than in the old, so the
artificial flies should also be large and gaudy:
and, if the angler be not artist enough to tie
his own flies, and wishes to provide himself
with a batch previously to visiting North
America, let him select those only which

would be preferred by the cockney sportsman.
All the lists of palmers, or, as old Izaac has
it, " the dun-fly, the stone-fly, the red-fly, the
moor-fly, the tawny-fly, the shell-fly, the
cloudy or blackish-fly, the flag-fly, the vine-
fly: there be—of flies, caterpillars, and canker-
flies, and bear-flies—and, indeed, too many
either for me to name or for you to remember," with their sober relations, the lake-flies,
may be left in the shop for the use of the
floggers of our hackneyed streams and lakes,
whose knowledge of the art has been derived
from a careful perusal of Izaac Walton or Sir
Humphrey Davy; or from dear-bought experience, which teaches discrimination between
the shades of the " copper," " mulberry," or
" purple claret " — the " pale " or " brown
cinnamon," or " sooty olive." Let the America bound fisherman then select those most
bedizened with gold tinsel, and made of the
brightest colours.

There is a saying among fishermen, "a bright

fly on a sunny day," "a dark one for a cloudy day"—but in America both salmon and trout will at all times and in all waters prefer the most brilliant.

[1] An angler, of great experience, pointed out the above passage to me, and said that, "although he perfectly agreed with me, and was convinced that *all practical fishermen* would be of the same opinion, he had remarked a direct contradiction in many of the works on angling." I therefore took the trouble to look over several; from which I give, on one side, opinions which bear out my statement, and afterwards those which contradict it.

PRO.

1. It is a general rule by all practical fishermen whom I know, that, so far as it can be followed, a *dark fly* must be fished upon a *cloudy day*, a bright one on a sunny day; and for this simple reason, that on dark and gloomy days dark flies are to be found on the water, and *vice versa*.

2. If the water be full, and *somewhat coloured*, your flies may be of the larger and *darker kind;* if, on the contrary, the water should be *low* and *clear*, and the *day*

CON.

1. A *darker fly*, with the wings formed of the feathers of a starling, or a bald coote, &c., will also be found of service when the day is *rather bright*, and the water clear. — *Stephen Oliver's Recollections of Fly-fishing, in Westmoreland, &c.*, p. 110.

2. Should the clouds disappear and it become *bright*, change your flies for *darker* ones.—*Sir H. Davy. Salmonia*, p. 112.

I will mention a circum-

For salmon the more gaudy the better—bright orange bodies, and a brilliant blue are always good. These colours imitate the natural dragon-flies of the country. Golden pheasant is sure everywhere.

bright, your fly should be dressed accordingly.—*Hofland's Anglers' Manual*, p. 205.

stance which every accomplished fly-fisher ought to know—putting the *dark* flies on for the *bright* gleams of the sun, and the *gaudy* flies *when* the *dark* clouds appear.—*Ibid.* p. 137.

3. The author of the "Hints for Fly-fishers," published in "The Sporting Review" for April, 1841, states, after quoting the above, in direct contradiction of Younger's and of Stodart's views on the same subject, "the two last quotations seem to be contradictory of the first, and go to the very opposite extreme of Mr. Hofland, and equally *wide of the true principle*."—*S.R.*, v., 270.

3. And note also, that the *light* fly does usually make most sport in a *dark* day ; and the darkest and least fly in a *bright or clear* day.—*Izaac Walton*, p. 184.

4. Small *light* - coloured flies are for *clear* waters and *clear* atmospheres; large, *dark* - *coloured* flies when

4. The sun proves *cloudy:* then must you set forth either your ground bait tackles, or of the *brightest* of

For the large sea trout of the Gulf of St. Lawrence, when fishing in tide-ways or at the mouths of harbours, the flies must be very large and gaudy, and should be tied with natural scarlet feathers, (no scarlet dye is so bright when wet,) obtained from the tail-feathers of the gray parrot, or those of the scarlet tanager (*tanagra rubra*). I do not, however, mean to recommend that the fisher-man should go about visiting with a pair of pincers in his pocket, in order to harass old ladies by his cruelty in extracting the

vice versa.—Best's Art of Angling, p. 140.

your flies. If the sun proves *bright* and clear, then must you put on the darkest of your flies, thus must you to work with your flies, light for darkness, and dark for lightness.—*Thomas Baker's Art of Angling*, p. 140.

N.B. The best rule is to fish the flies upon the water, and for which Nature will furnish the examples to be imitated: by a close examination it will be found that, on dark and cloudy days, dark flies are to be found on the water, and vice versa. He who fishes by rule and not after Nature is no fly-fisher.

said feathers from their pet birds; but when fairly obtained they are good. Should he have the opportunity of getting those of the "curry curry," or South American Curlew, he will obtain a still more brilliant colour than that of either the scarlet tanager or those feathers contained in Poll's tail. No natural scarlet can rival it, except perhaps the topknot of the ivory-billed woodpecker, the feathers of which are admirably adapted to match as hackles. The flies should be ribbed with a liberal quantity of large *round* gold thread, until they become entirely scarlet and gold, and so long as a particle of the feather or tinsel remains on the hook they will continue to kill.

For trout fishing, for the above stated reason, viz., the size of the insects, " river flies," so termed in England, are absolutely useless; the fish in New Brunswick will not look at them. Good-sized " lake flies," and those only of the brightest colours, will have any chance.

The difficulty of obtaining any information about the mystery of dyeing is very great; it is not to be expected that the shopkeeper, whose existence in many cases depends on his skill in the art, will disclose the secret whereby a particular process of making a certain colour may be known, and by these means get into the hands of his rival in trade. And if perchance a person, by dint of bribery, flatters himself that he has obtained the secret, in all probability there is some item in the receipt omitted, which gives it a peculiar shade different from the original—the least difference being fatal to the fly. One story, *apropos* to this nicety of shade.

There lives in an humble cottage on the shore of Clonave, a character well known to most of the floggers of the Westmeath lakes; and few there are of them, when fishing Lough Dereverragh, who have not paid a visit to Matty Blake, to obtain, with the silver hook, that addition to their basket, which may make up the deficiency of their own skill, or prevent a laugh at going home empty—and on a day when the inmates of the more aristocratic boats take drift after drift, and change over from shore to shore, Matty's "*cot*" may be seen taking short "falls" under Clonave or Derragh; and the boatmen of the former, who have not been able to shout "cookoo," have repeatedly called attention, exclaiming, "Matty's in a fish." The interior economy of his cot is delightful. It is flat-bottomed, as are all of this sort of craft; and that it was watertight no one could gainsay, from the fact of sundry pieces of turf floating about in the bottom; at one end, under some grass and flaggers are generally from eight to ten fish, nearly as broad as they are long, and in weight varying from three to eight pounds; at the other a thick piece of the root of a flagger is lying on one of the natural knees of oak (which serve to keep the fabric together), into which piece of flagger are stuck the different flies, and various shades of the green drake, which Matty has from time to time tried upon his casting-line.[1]

Matty Blake's forte, however, lies in his success in dyeing a particular shade of colour called the "sooty olive," and for his skill in *fixing* the *yellow* dye, so necessary in matching the natural colour of the "green drake." Whether he has any midnight dealings with the banshees, who are said to hold their revels under the hawthorn bushes of Kiltoom, is not known, or in the ruined vaults of Mortimer's Castle, where

> " Fairies, by moonlight, oft are seen,
> Tripping round the smooth sward green ;
> Her beams reflected from the wave,
> Afford the light their revels crave."

[1] The lake fishermen may take " a wrinkle" from this ; for, instead of being obliged to return your flies *wet* into the box or book, or to stick them into your hatband— from the latter of which you can only extract them by means of a knife or pair of scissors, and having when required from either of the former, some half dozen scattered about by the winds, you will find it much more convenient, to say nothing of the tax on your patience, when the fish

Some there are, however, who affirm that it
is from a particular kind of peat, otherwise turf, that he extracts his celebrated
" sooty ;" and that in the well smoke-dried
thatch of Matty's cabin on Clonave lies the
whole secret.   Be that as it may, there is no
such colour to be found elsewhere—and Matty
keeps his secret inviolate.   But to my story.

It so happened that a friend of mine, who
had often paid a visit to Matty's " cabin," for
the purpose of buying flies, was fishing on
Lough Dereverragh, and, in spite of his smart
rod and well-appointed boat, could not raise
a fish or a " *cookoo*" ; [1] and observing that
from the humble cot they were constantly
thrusting out a landing-net, and as constantly
securing a fine fish, our friend went alongside,

are " mad up" and dashing at " the drake," to be able to
extract the fly you wish to put upon your casting-line in
an instant from the pulpy substance of the flaggers.

[1] " Cookoo" is the shout of emulation given by the
boatmen on the Westmeath waters, to announce that " the
fish" is in the "landing-net."

and asked "on what shade of the drake they were killing?" "On *the yolly buff*, plaise your honour," was the reply. My friend tried all the shades of yellow buff he possessed, not forgetting "the monkey;" and, although the fish were "mad up," and dashing at the drakes, as they freed themselves from their cases, and struggled forth on their flight over the water; and although the trout were swallowing them in dozens, as their wings got entangled in the streaks of froth, still he could not "stir" a fish; and finally went in for luncheon at a rude pier made of huge stones on the shore of Clonave.

After indulging in pigeon-pies, mayonaise of chicken, cold punch and "a weed," Matty's cot came alongside, in one end of which was reared his rod, and upon the casting-line, as an upper dropper, hung the identical "yolly buff," which had done so much execution in the morning. Matty extended himself on the green turf, for which his locale is famed, and

waited an expected change in the weather—
the fish having suddenly "gone down." My
friend entered into conversation, and began
an examination of Matty's "foot link," and
contrived to detach from it the "*yolly*
buff;" he then jumped into his boat, and
desired his men to "give way," at the same
time chucking half a crown to Matty, as he
called out that he was "sold," and that *now*
it was *his turn*. Matty very quietly replied,
"Yer honour's welcome to it; they're off
the 'yolly buff' for this sason; and after those
bloody white clouds pass over, about half past
three, they'll 'be mad up' on the pale shade
of the '*dirty* buff.' "

The Indians have the means of staining
porcupine's quills, moosehair, or wood for
baskets of very brilliant colours, but these
they keep strictly secret. Mr. Perley, of New
Brunswick, tried, but in vain, to learn their
processes; and, as he did not succeed, it is unlikely they will ever be discovered. The
preparations are considered sacred, and the

slightest information has never been known to be given on the subject. A few receipts are given below, which, after much pains and many experiments, have been found to turn out in general clear, bright, and true; and those most appropriate for the North American waters, such as the ambers, different shades of blue, green, scarlet, blood-red, and gold, are marked with an asterisk. The more sober colours, such as the cinnamons, browns, and olives, instead of being entirely omitted, are left on the chance of their being useful to the home-bound fisherman. And by steeping the fur or feathers intended to be dyed in a solution of alum, previously to putting them into the colouring liquid, they will be sufficiently *fixed*, and will not fade.

One word as to the best material for making body or dubbing. First of all, not only as the most brilliant and clear when held up to light, is the fur of the white seal; but in the water, which is of much the most importance, it is the most lively and transparent of any kind of fur. Next comes pig's down; and last and worst, mohair, which becomes so sodden and dead in the water as never to be used, except in the case of not being able to obtain either of the former.

N.B. Should you, after dyeing any colour, find that it does not please you, or that it has faded, do not cast away the stuff; for, by simply boiling the dyed hair in alum water, it is a singular fact, that the mordant which holds the dye has the peculiar property of obliterating it; and thus much useless waste, often of a precious material, is avoided.

DYEING COLOURS FOR ARTIFICIAL FLIES.

All furs, hackles, feathers, &c., previously to being put into any dyeing liquor, must be prepared in alum water (except such dyeing liquor as may have vitriol in it).

BLACK.—Two ounces of logwood; half an ounce of shumach, boiled a sufficient time in half a pint of water; wet the stuff, put it in and boil it well; take it up and cool it; return it, and boil it again; take it up again and cool it; then add one ounce of copperas; boil it again sufficiently.

OLIVE.—Two ounces of fustic; half an ounce of logwood; boil well; put in the stuff after wetting; boil all well; take it up to cool; add one ounce of copperas; return it, and boil it sufficiently.

BROWN.—1. Three ounces of redwood; two ounces of fustic; boil it well: let it cool; put in the stuff after wetting; boil it well; take it up, and cool it; put in one ounce of copperas; return the stuff, and take your colour.

2. Two ounces and a half of logwood; five ounces and two drams of fustic; half an ounce of shumach; three ounces of copperas; half an ounce of alum; three ounces of redwood.

*DEEP BLUE.—1. Indigo, dissolved in warm water, with a mixture of vitriol.

2. Fourpennyworth of arsenic, dissolved by boiling a quart of water for one hour; dip the feathers or furs, and the oftener repeated the deeper the dye.

3. Add a little logwood and copperas for a brown.

N.B. Let this liquor cool before it is used.

*GREEN.—Threepennyworth of Spanish indigo (pulverized); two ounces of oil of vitriol; mix together; put a small proportion of this mixture into warm water, boiling hot for a light blue; a greater quantity for a middle-coloured blue; and a still greater quantity for a deep-coloured blue. Turmeric, added in small quantity, will produce a shade of green.

*BLOOD RED is made, first, by steeping in madder: second by steeping in Brazilwood. Should the colour be thought too high, dilute with urine.

*YELLOW may be dyed in the following manner: with turmeric, or the bark of the crab-apple tree.

Sooty Olive.—1. One pennyworth of fustic, two
ounces of turmeric; boil the fustic, and steep the hackles
therein when milk-warm.

2. Boil the turmeric and steep the hackles therein (pigs'
fur may be boiled in this). This dye will produce the
following shades, viz:—brown olive, sooty olive, yellow
and gold.

N.B. The hackles to make sooty olive must be a natural
black, and the hackles to make a brown must be a
natural red.

*Orange.—*Oranetto* for an orange colour. Steep the
hackles when boiling hot.

*Gold Colour.—1. First dip in fustic, boiling hot, wash
in cold water, then dip in turmeric boiling hot. The natural black hackles with this dye will make a sooty olive,
the red a brown one.

2. To dye red and black hackles a beautiful amber.
Steep them in one pennyworth of fustic and one pennyworth of the best indigo.

3. Take a small teacupful of ground or powdered
fustic, let it boil gently in more than half a pint of pure
water, dissolving one pennyworth of Spanish indigo, and
pour it into the fustic; let all boil together slowly; put into
this red, black, or any hackles, and after ten minutes all
will be dyed.

The red hackles will become a beautiful amber, the
black a colour bordering on amber, the gray a trans-
parency very beautiful. Hares' ear may be dyed in the
same manner.

To dye crimson hackles.—Having prepared the hackles
first in alum water, that they may hold the dye, boil them
in madder till they have absorbed a considerable quantity
of the dyeing matter; then wash them thoroughly, and

boil them in a separate vessel with cochineal, (an earthen vessel is better than a saucepan) and when you have dyed the hackles well in this, add a very small quantity of copperas to clear the shade. This shade can be darkened *ad libitum* by the addition of more copperas till you have as many as you fancy.

*YELLOW.—Dyers' weed or rocket, so called, will afford a beautiful yellow. This plant is very common, and is to be found in meadows, pastures, walls, and barren uncultivated places.[1]

Magnificent as is the fly-fishing in New Brunswick, it is not without its *desagremens*. Clouds of countless insects beset the face, hands, or any exposed parts of the piscator. Persons there are, it is true, who are not annoyed by mosquitoes, which here abound. But against the attacks of a small species of black gnat or sand-fly, even the tough skin of the Indian is not proof. These fasten on the forehead and behind the ears, and cut like a knife: to keep them off is impossible. By anointing themselves with the fat of pork or bear's grease, the Indians contrive to keep themselves free from their venom. But the white man suffers dreadfully.

[1] Reseda Luteola. (Irish buigh mor.)

Camphorated olive oil, with a few drops of oil of almonds, or any other bitter oil added, is recommended. No one should go into the woods in the fly season without a small pot of this mixture; for, should his patience be exhausted by the repeated applications necessary during the time he may be intent on beguiling the finny tribe, when he lays himself down to rest at night, it will tend much to allay the pain and inflammation caused by the sting of insects, and he will be sure to thank his stars that he possesses such a luxury.

CHAPTER VIII.

NOVA SCOTIA—A FORTNIGHT IN BUSH.

I really do think there is no luxury equal to that of
lying before a good fire on a good spruce bed, after a good
supper and a hard moose, chase in a fine clear frosty moonlight starry night.

LORD E. FITZGERALD.

While round, in brutal jest, were thrown
The half-gnawed rib and marrow-bone.

MARMION.

The Start—Annapolis—Micmac Village—Flappers—
Trout—Lakes—Rivers—Still Waters—Tracks—Moose—
The Death—Potatoes—Indigestion—Turtle—Lampreys
—Stone Pipes—Calling the Moose—Emperor of China.

Rifles, guns, fishing-rods, blankets, axes,
tomahawks, salt pork, biscuits, and a couple
of birch-canoes, the whole under the charge
of Francis Glode, a Micmac Indian, were put
on board the steamer for Annapolis; and, all

the preparations for a fortnight's sojourn "in bush" being completed, Captain E— and myself started from St. John's, in the month of August, to hunt the moose in Nova Scotia. On nearing the coast, the land loomed in the most extraordinary manner, and masses of trees of a gigantic growth hung suspended, as it were, in the heavens. The Wicklow mountains may at times be seen to loom in the same way long after losing sight of the Irish coast; or, as poor Power would have said, "after you had seen it *clane* out of sight."

The bay of Annapolis is landlocked on either side by the iron-bound coast of Nova Scotia, and the entrance to it through straits wooded to the water's edge is most striking; the canoes of the Micmac Indians, hunting the porpoise, which covered the water at the time, added not a little to the picturesque effect. Suddenly the bay opened, and, after an hour's steaming, the "Maid of the Mist" landed us at Annapolis, where we were joined by the chief of the tribe, Charles Glode, (our guide's brother,) and another Indian, supposed to be the most accomplished moose-hunter in the province ; he spoke no language but that of his nation, was a fine athletic fellow, and lived entirely by the produce of the chase.

The result of a consultation was, that we were to strike the head-waters of a river about ten miles south of Annapolis, and follow it through a chain of lakes until it finally emptied itself into the Atlantic below Halifax. The hunting ground once settled, the Indians shouldered the provisions, and, placing the canoes on their heads, went off at a long trot, and we, who had only our rifles to carry, found quite enough to do to keep pace with them.

An Indian path led to a Micmac village of some twelve or fourteen lodges, where they halted for their hunting-knives, toma-hawks, and other necessary apparatus for the chase ; and we smoked the pipe with their squaws.

> Happy mortal! he who knows
> Pleasure which a pipe bestows.
> Curling eddies climb the room,
> Wafting round a mild perfume.

On leaving the village, we struck directly into the woods, following in Indian file. On reaching the first lake, it was found necessary to stanch the canoes before launching, an operation easily performed by applying lighted torches of bark to the gum and resin with which the seams are covered ; when melted sufficiently, the Indian wetted his thumb, (in the manner most convenient to himself,) and plastered the resin anew over the seams. That finished, we paddled across a lake, crossed a portage, and halted for the night on the shores of the second lake ; and, whilst the Indians were making the camp, a stream close by, full of trout, came most *apropos* for supper. Trout thus fresh caught and fried

with salt pork are excellent, and any one who
has hunted in the woods of North America
can also appreciate a kettle of boiling hot
tea ; so refreshing after fatigue, and doubly
so on the first day, when fresh from a town
life, and before condition has given full play
to the muscles.

In the middle of the night we were
awakened by the most mournful and painful
shrieks, as though a woman was suffering
torture, and screaming for assistance. It
was the cry of " the Loon," or " Great Northern Diver." They make these noises when
alarmed by the sight of bears. One of the
Indians snatched up a rifle and disappeared ;
he returned towards morning, but without
having got a shot. The Indians can imitate the
cry of the loon, and, by concealing themselves
in the brushwood on the edges of the lakes,
and waving their hats, will call them within
shot, but they dive so instantaneously, that
the click of a copper cap, or a flash in the

pan, is sufficient to give them warning, and they are under water before the shot can reach them. But by suddenly jumping up with a great noise, you may alarm the bird, when his first impulse will be to open his wings for flight—his second to dive; then is the moment to catch him. But, unless you are very close to him, he will carry off a large charge of shot.

The following morning, several lakes and portages were crossed in a thick fog. On its suddenly clearing off, we found ourselves in a beautiful lake covered with islands or rather huge rocks of granite and porphyry, of all manner of fantastic shapes and forms; and in the midst of several broods of flappers (young wood ducks [1]). The Indians were instantly all excitement; off they set in chase, straining every nerve, the canoes flying through the water at a most astonishing rate. The flappers dived whenever closed upon,

[1] Dendronessa sponsa.

until, after two hours of paddling and ma-
nœuvring, some six or eight were caught. No
bad things for supper, when hunger does duty
for Cayenne pepper and Harvey sauce.

The broad outlet from this lake being
broken up into a succession of rapids, the
skill of the Indians was put to the test, and
the canoes often made tremendous lurches,
plunging head-foremost into whirlpools; but
the Indians, ever on the alert, fended off and
preserved their equilibrium apparently without effort.

An Indian never does an awkward thing—
when hunting, he never steps upon dry twigs,
or any thing likely to alarm the ears of the
most watchful animal—he moves without
noise—he looks before him, behind him, and
from right to left, at every step—he observes
the patches of moss, any peculiarity or
marked feature, the trees and their branches,
which he invariably recognises, should he
cross them again.   In his canoe he is equally

on the look-out; along the shore, or in, or
under the water, nothing escapes his notice;
his paddle propels his canoe without noise or
splash; his carriage, his manners, and his
movements, are all grace, all ease, because
they are natural.

This river was full of large trout, and the
merry salmo huko of Sir Humphrey Davy,
which, when hooked, jump to the height of
four or five feet out of the water. There
was also a large species of char, averaging
from one to three pounds, as broad and thick
as they were long, their bellies of a deep gold
colour, covered with blood-red spots—excellent to eat, playing very strong, and affording
undeniable sport to the angler. So eager
would they rise, that five or six would race
at the flies at the same time, and would continue to do so, when wings, body, hackles
and all were completely stripped off the
hooks; I caught a fine fish of three pounds
weight, attracted by the " ghost of a fly," a

mere bit of tinsel, the only remnant of what
had been a mulberry claret, and had done
execution in Ireland, when the drake " was
upon" Lough Dereverragh; in fact, they would
rise at any thing moving through the water.
The rivers teemed with fish; and, as we could
catch any number, we made a few casts into
each eddy where the largest fish lay, and
which invariably rose first. It was impossible to fish from the banks, they were so
overshadowed by the forest; we were, therefore, obliged to cast the flies from our canoes,
and it required no little skill to kill three
large trout which were constantly upon one's
casting-line at the same time, and that when
sitting in a birch-canoe in a rapid river.

Occasionally we could land upon a rock, or
large stone, and fish the pools from thence,
but it was a slippery operation at best, and
could not always be effected. But the fishing was excellent, and flies had never
been cast in these streams before. As every

thing in the New World is on the mammoth scale, so are the insects—the large flies used upon the Westmeath lakes are the correct size and exactly the thing, both in New Brunswick and Nova Scotia. But the wear and tear of tackle is great. I had, luckily, materials for making them. The tying amused the Indians not a little, and to them the whole operation of fly-fishing was a source of great curiosity and delight.

The ends of the moose-wood bitten off, the brushwood broken and trampled down, the water-lilies pulled up and in part eaten, and the numbers of fresh tracks, were certain signs of moose being in the immediate neighbourhood; it was, therefore, deemed imprudent to light fires or make a camp. The canoes, turned over, afforded sufficient covering for our heads, but the night was cold and we were obliged to forego our kettle of tea, most sensibly felt as the greatest privation after a hard day's fag. We started at daylight next morning, but in a fog, paddling carefully along the " still waters."

These " still waters," so called by the Indians, are boggy creeks of the great lakes and rivers, and where the water is stagnant : between them and the forests on either side is a luxuriant growth of bog myrtle, dog-wood, moose-wood, Labrador-tea, and wild roses, the resort of bittern [1] and the water-fowl tribe. Through these it is the moose's great delight to wade and suck the water-lilies ; it was in the hopes of thus surprising them when entangled in the brushwood and up to their bellies in the water, that we had made so early a start, and had preserved such profound silence. But the wind was unfavourable, and we had the mortification to find that

[1] The American bittern is much smaller than the European species, and its note is totally unlike the loud booming cry of the latter. It is a night bird, and its sight is most acute during the evening twilight. When disturbed, it rises with a heavy and awkward flight, uttering the cry, " *kwa ! kwa !*"

we had only disturbed them—but even this was attended with no small excitement. Soon after hunting the " still waters," we entered a great lake, the largest of the chain, called by the Indians the Lake of the Nightingales; and made straight for a sand-bank in the midst of it, with the intention of lighting a fire, having a kettle of hot tea and a good breakfast after the fasting and cold of the previous night.   This shoal had been selected as the least likely place to alarm the moose—but upon landing, there was not wherewithal to make a fire, and two of the Indians were despatched in search of wood and birch bark.

After they had been gone for some time, and the sun had nearly dispelled the fog, we were suddenly put on the *qui vive* by shouts reverberating through the woods, when presently we saw a great splashing in the lake, and above it, looming in the haze, a dark mass towering into the clouds—it might be a water-spout; our Indian thought the shouts proceeded from a gang of lumberers; when, in a moment, I found myself seized by the herculean chief of the Micmacs, and literally chucked into the canoe. My companion and the rifles were treated in the same manner; and, before we had breathing time to recover the surprise, we were going "Derby pace" down the lake, and the Indian, straining every nerve, paddled with such force that the canoe was nearly buried in her own way.

For some time the hallooing and yelling continued, until at last the mystery was cleared up, and we discovered a huge moose in the water; driven into it by the other Indians, who had shouted to attract our attention. Both canoes now bore down upon him at right angles. Two men in a canoe can always propel it faster than a moose can swim, but both canoes were a long way off—we had but one man in ours, and a stern chase is always a long one, so say the nautical world; however, we arrived at a point of the main land just as the animal

had landed. A few seconds and we should have
lost him: we arrived in the nick of time,
however, and he dashed off at full speed. I
fired. The ball passed through his heart;
he made a tremendous bound straight up into
the air, and fell upon his back, dead. It was
a noble animal, seventeen hands high. A
second moose had been seen on the island
whence they had driven the one already
bagged, and, my companion being anxious to
shoot it, we went off in pursuit, and after a
similar chase he succeeded.

The Lake of the Nightingales being evidently the resort of moose; the inlets and
outlets full of fish; the beauty of the spot to
which the chase had accidentally led us, and
the Indians being ravenous to devour the
meat, all led us to determine to make it head-
quarters. A camp was accordingly constructed in orthodox Indian fashion, and long
poles were placed across to dry the venison
upon. Sabbattis proceeded with great glee

to skin and cut up the moose, and, before a fire could be lit, commenced devouring the raw flesh, without bread or salt, and, when cooked, they all ate of it until they literally could not stir. Like pike, they will gorge themselves, and then sleep or rest until hunger again drives them forth in search of food.

The moofle, a lump of fat about the nose of the moose, is esteemed a great delicacy by epicures. This we reserved for ourselves, together with the bones, from which, by roasting in the fire, we obtained the most delicious marrow, excellent when eaten with dried biscuits. The meat is the best of all wild venison, and the tongues are as good as those of the reindeer. These were hung up to dry, and reserved for our friends in the old world.

As the Indians had over-eaten themselves to such a degree that their locomotive powers were any thing but dubious, we gave their digestion four-and-twenty hours to recover, and occupied ourselves in fishing and reconnoitring the forest, where, for the first time, we saw the potato in its natural state, growing in stringy bunches about the roots of the spruce firs; but they were bitter and unpalatable, generally about the size of a filbert, and not exceeding that of a walnut. Some of the pines were enormous; at least two hundred feet high; perfectly straight, and would square three. The total absence of the white cedar (so common in every swamp in New Brunswick) surprised me: and it is worthy of remark that, although the boundary between the two provinces is not a natural but merely an imaginary one, yet, that line once crossed into Nova Scotia, the cedar ceases to be found.[1] Neither are the deer, so common in New Brunswick, to be met with in the other province, to the Indians of which

---

[1] The Bluenoses declare that branches of this cedar placed amongst clothes or furs will keep off moths.

they are wholly unknown; and, on one occasion, when I had taken Francis out hunting with me in New Brunswick, he ran after one for the best part of the day on snow-shoes, and came back remarkably sulky at not having got a *sight* of it.

The Milicete Indians declare that these deer will not cross the St. John's river.

The stomachs of the Indians having had a liberal four-and-twenty hours' rest, my companion repaired to the " still waters," where he got nine shots at moose in the one day; and I, accompanied by John, carrying a quarter of a moose on his back, went half a day's journey to a settlement, where, as he expected, we exchanged the meat for salt sufficient to preserve the skin for stuffing. We got, likewise, a mess of potatoes, much prized by them *medicinally* after a moose debauch, as on this occasion.

The Indians did not wish us to kill more moose, nor would it have been sportsmanlike

so to do, as we could make no use of the
meat; but it was often tantalizing when,
suddenly descending a rapid, they would swing
the canoes round, hold them fast with their
poles, and point to a huge moose, who would
take himself off at a long trot. On one occasion, however, the temptation was too great,
and a ball from my rifle passed through the
ear of one. So quick-sighted are the Indians,
that all three at the same moment exclaimed,
" It has gone through his ear."

These Indians carve pipes out of a porous
kind of stone (soap-stone) found in the beds
of torrents, and called by them pipe-stones;
it is soft, works well, and resembles the green
lava of Vesuvius. During the intervals between repletion and the chase, Sabbattis
made one, which I still possess; it is exqui-
sitely finished. On the front of the bowl, in
alto-relievo, is a deer's head and horns; on
the reverse and either side, Indians' head, the
character of which, and the accompanying

ornaments, are decidedly Egyptian. I was much struck on finding the same ornaments, frieze, and even the same character of heads, in one of the tombs lately discovered in the Necropolis of the Tarquinii, near Cornetto.

The outlet of the lake was full of lampreys in their migration from the sea, lying in coils upon beds of sand which they throw up themselves; and they were so thick that, upon lowering a stick with some hooks attached to it, and jerking it up suddenly, three or four were pulled out at a time. In the shoal parts of the lake, we speared terrepins, a large kind of fresh-water turtle, of a beautiful sea-green colour, weighing from six to eight pounds, and full of eggs, much esteemed by the Indians, which were not bad roasted.

The Indians having despatched three or four dozen of lampreys, though without the bad effect which is said to have followed a like excess on the part of one of our early kings, and imitating ourselves the resignation

of the guardsman, who made up his mind,
before he embarked for Egypt, that he could
rough it upon a beefsteak and a bottle of
claret, we contrived to do the like on an excellent supper of venison, grouse, turtles' eggs,
and a dish of fish; and, having lit our pipes,
and stretched our feet towards a roaring fire,
we might truly say with Goldsmith,

> Oh, luxury! thou curse by Heaven's decree,
> How ill-exchanged are things like these for thee!

John gave the following description of the
manner of "calling the moose," which takes
place about the end of September or beginning
of October, when the frosts have set in. As
fires cannot be lit, nor tobacco smoked, this
species of hunting is attended with great
privation and hardship. Then is the rutting
season; the antlers of the male have attained
their full growth; and he is in truth a noble
animal. When the moon is at its full, the
Indians proceed with the greatest caution to
the still waters, and take up a position in their

canoes amongst the adjacent brushwood. They are provided with a piece of birch-bark, rolled up into the shape of a speaking-trumpet, by blowing through which they imitate exactly the lowing made by the female when in expectation of a partner.

John described it as glorious, when perfect stillness reigned over the forest, to hear the bulls, sometimes three or four together, first at a long distance, and by degrees nearer and nearer, rushing on, bellowing and roaring, knocking each other over, trampling down the brushwood, and dashing through the streams, until they come so close to the hunter, that they have no time to discover the deception, before a ball from the unerring aim of an Indian's rifle stretches them lifeless.[1]

[1] From Father Repas' account of his residence at the court of Pekin, we find that the Emperor of China amused himself by "calling" deer much in the manner practised by the Indians in Nova Scotia; he says, p. 79,

" The Emperor took part in another species of sport unknown in Europe. He set out by night with all the great company above mentioned, and, when within two miles of the spot selected for the sport, he left the army and ascended the top of the hill with six or seven hunters clothed in stag-skins from head to foot. Here one of the hunters put on a kind of mask, resembling a stag's head with horns, and concealed himself among the bushes, in such a manner that at first sight he might be taken for a stag, while the emperor and the others crouched down close by, all being armed with good guns, to the end of which were fixed small pieces of stag's horn. The stags are followed by several does, which they will not allow any other stag to approach. Early in the morning, they instinctively raise a cry of challenge; the other stags arrive, and a fight ensues, which continues until one is slain, when the victor takes possession of his rival's herd of does. One of the hunters now blows an instrument which both in shape and sound very much resembles those with which our herdsmen call the swine, and which closely imitates the belling of the stag. At this sound the stags hasten to the hill, and seeking their supposed rival, they come within gun-shot and meet with their death."

CHAPTER IX.

A RACE THROUGH THE UNITED STATES.

" Sir, our pills!!!"—*A Yankee naval officer introduces the assistant surgeon.*

Star-bespangled banner—Flying Artillery—Crimping System—Table d'Hôtes—Whales and Peas—Mercantile Fowls — Sea Speculations — Sky-blue —Yankee's Shaving—Frigid Baptists—Canals—Ontario.

The novelty of a New Brunswick life having a little worn off, three of us started, about the end of August, for a race through the northern States, as far as the Falls of Niagara. The steamer to which we consigned ourselves passed through the Bay of Passamaquoddy, the waters of which, studded with a thousand islands of all shapes and sizes, are beyond description beautiful. Eastport, a frontier town of the State of Maine, was our first landing-place. Over the fort floated the star-bespangled banner, at least half an acre of bunting—" The stars to illumine our friends, the stripes to punish our enemies."

This fort was garrisoned by a *company* of horse artillery. It was composed entirely of deserters from our regiments quartered from time to time in New Brunswick. These regiments being infantry, the men had, of course, never learned to ride, and rarely to exercise great guns. Nevertheless, they did duty as flying artillery in the United States. They wore fancy-coloured waistcoats under sky-blue jackets, trowsers of the same colour, with broad yellow stripes down them; their boots turned up at the toes, like skates, the trowsers only reaching half way down their legs. The whole was crowned by a frightful leather cap, with a huge brass letter to denote their company; but it is only fair to remark that their barracks were as clean as an unlimited allowance of whitewash could make them.

We recognised a rascal who had deserted from St. John's not long before. He was walking about, dragging a nine-pound shot fastened to his leg (by which we concluded that he had already got into a scrape), smoking a cigar, and looking as if he did not care a d—n for General Jackson or any one else. We heard, soon after we left Eastport, that, this company having been ordered to Florida, to quell an insurrection of the Seminole Indians, the majority of them deserted on their march to Boston. They were, however, retaken, and sent on. Upon my return to New Brunswick, I saw a letter from the last of the survivors to his brother, recommending him and his comrades on no account to desert their colours for the American service, he being the only one who had escaped the toma-hawk of the Indians, or the deadly pestilence of the swamps.

The difficulty, however, of preventing de-sertion was, in spite of all warnings, very great in New Brunswick. Yankee agents followed the men, enticed them into crimping houses, and plied them with drink, and, when sufficiently intoxicated, they were put on board fast-sailing schooners, which got under weigh whilst they lay in a state of unconsciousness. On coming to themselves, many might have returned, had they not been plied with more rum, and dreaded the consequences of their first transgression. There was but one instance of a man's returning in the two years we remained in New Brunswick.

The officers of the United States' army, whom we met at Eastport, from having seen much of Indian life, were very agreeable; and the commandant, in particular, who had served in the Far West, was a most gentlemanlike man. His daughter, a young lady of fourteen, understood Latin and Greek, and was looking forward to her return to school at Boston to learn Hebrew, and finish her education.

The steamers to Portland had blown up, or

been burnt, so we were obliged to go round in a schooner, on board of which there were the most dreadful set I ever recollect to have encountered. One man got up at table to let another pass down, who immediately dropped into the vacant place. The civil man remonstrated—in vain; the answer he received was, " Well, I guess you shouldn't have got up then—Hell—I shall keep it now." After dinner, the majority sang psalms, until dispersed by a drunken slumberer singing " Yankee Doodle," and " Hail, Columbia."

It was midnight when we landed at Portland. After going the round of the hotels, which were full, we discovered a large reception room, filled with " shake-downs," in one of which we found a fellow-passenger already ensconced. He had turned in with all his clothes on, as he had done during the three nights on board the schooner, what the Yankees term " all standing," viz., in boots, great coat, &c. He had besides heaped the clothes from all the other beds on his own, though the room was hot to suffocation; of these, however, we soon dispossessed him, and betook ourselves to horizontal refreshment in the best manner we could.

We were much struck with Portland, which is a very neat town : double rows of trees on each side of the streets; the houses clinker-built, and painted in bright colours, divided from the street and each other by gardens and parterres. From the top of the Observatory, there is a grand view, commanding the town, harbour, and its islands, and Mount Washington, a bold hill, in shape resembling Soracte, bounding the horizon to the north-east.

The ladies were well dressed, well *chausséd*, and well *coifféd à la chinoise*, with a well-gummed *créve-cœur* in front of the ear, domestically termed by them a " spit curl."

For the first time we here dined at a regular American *table d'hôte*. The consumption of food was fearful; some left the table in seven minutes and a half; from that to fourteen the room was cleared, and we were left alone. Boiled green Indian corn, plaistered over with butter, seemed the favourite dish, and most excellent it was. They held it at both ends, gnawing it round, ridge after ridge, like a man playing pandean pipes. Some, in their hurry, transfixed whole fowls and dragged them bodily on to their plates. One man, addressing me in mercantile phraseology, said, " Stranger, I guess I'll trouble you for the *balance* of that fowl," meaning what remained of it on the dish.

On another occasion, a brother officer, travelling with his wife, was dining at Boston, on the first day green peas made their appearance. He saw the dish making its rounds, and one man between himself, his wife, and the peas; he therefore made sure of getting some for her; but no—the brute having swept the whole contents of the dish into his plate, gave

the dish an exulting shove, and, turning round,
exclaimed, " I guess I'm a whale at peas, by
G—."[1]   It is painful to witness the unlady-
like practice of arranging peas along the blade
of a knife and eating them off by rows, at
once dispelling the charm of a young and
pretty face; nor was the substitution of forks
for toothpicks a redeeming trait.

[1] However, it is but justice to the Americans to state
that no later than at the close of the seventeenth century,
we find a *royal* " whale at peas."   A King of England (a
Dutchman, it is true,) of whom the Duchess of Marlborough, in her apology for her conduct, observes :—" I give
an instance of his vulgar behaviour at his own table, when
the Princess of Wales* dined with him.   It was in the
beginning of his reign, when she was with child of the Duke
of Gloucester.   There happened to be a plate of peas, the first
that had been seen that year.   The King, without offering
the Princess the least share of them, ate them every one
himself.   Whether he offered any to the Queen I cannot
say; but he might do so safely enough, for he knew she
durst not touch them.   The Princess confessed, when she
came home, she had so much mind to the peas, that she was
afraid to look at them, and yet could hardly keep her eyes
off them."

* His sister-in-law, the Princess of Denmark, afterwards
Queen Anne.

From Portland we embarked on board a magnificent steamer for Boston. There were upwards of four hundred persons on board, half of them ladies. The gentlemen's cabin was one hundred and eighty feet long. The doors of the ladies' cabin were left open, in consequence of the excessive heat. There were many unprovided with berths, and they lay about in beautiful confusion, most of them in great dishabille.

These steamers have much the appearance of floating bazaars, every sort of amusement going on, from eating, drinking, and gambling, to swapping and speculating, even to the taking advantage of the miseries of their fellow-passengers: it being a common practice, when the steamers are crowded and a rough passage expected, for individuals to take a number of berths on the chance of *sea-sick bidders*;—three, four, or even five times the original price being then given.

" The Tremont House," the crack hotel of
Boston and of the United States, was full, but
we were well put up in the "American," a
new house. We had now got fairly into
American hours—breakfast from seven to
eight, dinner from one to two, and tea six to
seven. Tea and coffee made the only distinction of the first and last, for meat was
equally served at all.

The bedsteads in the hotel fell to pieces on
touching a spring, an ingenious invention in a
town where fires so constantly occur. There
were no fewer than four on the night of our
arrival; but they are wonderfully soon got
under, the fire-engine department being well
organized.

> " But fires are getting fainter,
> Incendiarism's flat,
> For there's a clever painter
> Will put a stop to that.
> Though form'd of wood, he's shown
> Each house will 'scape all right;—
> He'll paint them so like stone,
> They will not catch alight!"

We lionized in due order the park, called the Common, full of magnificent old elms, of which the Bostonians take great care. We hired excellent hacks, and visited Mount Auburn, the cemetery of the aristocracy of Boston — Spurzheim is buried here — and returned through Cambridge, the largest college in the States, and by Bunker's Hill, where they have erected a monument to commemorate the battle which *we* won. Lafayette laid the foundation-stone. The ladies here are not so pretty as those of Portland, and the men are generally tall, but wretchedly ill-made, and, from the habit of stooping over their desks, become round-shouldered, have a slovenly gait, and the unmanly habit of shaving off their whiskers gives them a sky-blue or leaden appearance.

No independent Yankee ever thinks of shaving himself. They study the comfort of that operation much, and the chair in which they sit has a board or platform for the head to rest upon, which is raised or depressed by a screw to the desired height; when adjusted, the artist, generally a Negro, seizes the patient's nose between his forefinger and thumb, and shaves him *slick*. He then powders the face as a finale. We tried the process, and found it rather comfortable. At Eastport a woman operated. A New Englander travels so much, that a wardrobe would be in the way: he therefore gets everything "all standing," a complete suit, and when worn out he buys another; rarely has he a change of anything, with the exception of fronts, one of which, tied on after shaving, does duty for, and has all the appearance of, a clean shirt; but like Topffer's Monsieur Vieuxbois, "il change de linge bien rarement." His kit, therefore, not being extensive, packs easily into a small valise, and is conveniently carried in one hand; brushes, combs, toothbrushes, and round-towels being generally to be found suspended from the walls in most of the hotels and steamboats.

However, on this point nations differ materially; a Russian does not consider it dirty
to eat tallow candles or swallow train-oil. A
Jew condemns pork as unclean. A French
woman will not wash her face for fear of
spoiling her complexion. An Irish landlady
has been known to describe her lodger as
" The *claanest* jewel of a man in the world,
for, sure he wouldn't dirty a towel in a week;"
and the Spanish lady, the *chere amie* of an
officer at Gibraltar, whose teeth were suffering
in appearance from the use of cigarettes, was
presented by him with a tooth-brush. When
he called the next day, he found her busily
employed cleaning her trinkets with it. The
horror of one of Napoleon's generals was so
great on discovering that the object of his
affections, an Italian of high birth, never used
a certain description of bath, that on his
return to Paris, he caused a beautiful diminutive one of Sevres China, mounted with silver
legs, to be manufactured for her, and sent the

bijou with a well cacheted billet to *la bella principessa*, who, delighted with so novel a *cadeau*, but mistaking its use, asked a large circle of friends to dinner, and had a salad served up in it.

In the New England States, the ladies are for the most part extremely serious, and camp-meetings are more fashionable than theatres.

The 1st of June, 1813, was a day of no ordinary excitement at Boston. The rival frigates, the Shannon and the Chesapeake, were expected to come to an engagement on that very day. Everything was done that ingenuity could devise on the part of the American, Captain Lawrence, to bring his ship to the scratch in " tip-top" fighting trim. The crew were picked, four hundred and forty in number (exceeding that of his opponent by one hundred); further, he had the advantage in the weight of metal and the number of guns.

But so certain did the good folks of Boston

make of victory, that we were told they
actually prepared a magnificent *fête* for their
expected victorious countrymen, and the stairs
were left uncovered which led to the banquet-
ting-room, in order that the guests should
trample upon the prostrate British colours,
taken from the gallant Broke. For once,
however, Jonathan " reckoned without his
host." It must have been a brilliant sight—
happening, as it did, in sight of all Boston—
the known reputation of the commanders,
and their anxiety to meet in fair fight. In
fifteen minutes the affair was decided ; but I
quote a part of the despatch of the gallant
victor ; it is as concise and graphic as the feat
was gallantly performed.

" Shannon, Halifax, June 6, 1813.
" Sir,
        " I have the honour to inform you
that, being close in with Boston lighthouse,
in his Majesty's ship, under my command, on

the 1st inst., I had the pleasure of seeing that
the United States' frigate, Chesapeake, (whom
we had long been watching) was coming out
of the harbour to engage the Shannon; I took
a position between Cape Clear and Cape Cod,
and then hove-to for him to join us. The
enemy came down in a very handsome manner,
having three American ensigns flying; when,
closing with us, he sent down his royal yards.
I kept the Shannon's up, expecting the breeze
would die away. At half-past five, p.m., the
enemy hauled up within hail of us on the
starboard side, and the battle began, both
ships steering full under the topsails; after
exchanging between two and three broadsides,
the enemy's ship fell on board of us, her mizen
channels locking in with our fore-rigging. I
went forward to ascertain her position, and,
observing that the enemy were flinching from
their guns, I gave orders to prepare for
boarding. Our gallant band appointed to
that service immediately rushed in, under

their respective officers, upon the enemy's decks, driving everything before them with irresistible fury. The enemy made a desperate but disorderly resistance.

" The firing continued at all the gangways and between the tops, but, in two minutes' time, the enemy were driven, sword in hand, from every post. The American flag was hauled down, and the proud old British Union floated triumphant over it. In another minute they ceased firing from below, and called for quarter. The whole of this service was achieved in fifteen minutes from the commencement of the action. I have to lament the loss of many of my gallant shipmates, but they fell exulting in their conquest."

After giving a detailed but concise account of the gallant conduct of his respective officers and men, and but slightly hinting at a very severe wound received from a cutlass at the onset, when leading a party to attack some of the enemy, who had rallied on the forecastle, Captain Broke goes on to say :—

" The loss of the enemy was about seventy killed, and one hundred wounded. Among the former were four lieutenants, a lieutenant of marines, the master, and many other officers. Captain Lawrence is since dead of his wounds.

" The enemy came into action with a complement of 440 men. The Shannon, having picked up some recaptured seamen, had 330.

" The Chesapeake is a fine frigate, and mounts forty-nine guns, eighteens, on her main deck; thirty-twos on her quarter-deck and forecastle. Both ships came out of action in the most beautiful order, their rigging appearing as perfect as if they had only been exchanging a salute.

" I have the honour to be, &c.

(Signed)   " P. B. V. BROKE.[1]

" To Captain the Hon. J. Bladen Capel, &c. Halifax."

---

[1] Rear-Admiral Sir P. B. V. Broke, Bart., died January 3, 1841.

We quitted Boston, without regret, by the railroad for Worcester, which mode of travelling is designated by the Yankees "Hell in Harness." Owing to its serpentine construction, we progressed but slowly. The railway not being finished, we took the "stage" at Worcester. The stages in all parts of the United States are conducted on the same principle—abominable, cooped-up contrivances, holding nine inside, three on each seat, the centre one having a wide leather strap to support the backs of those who have the bad luck to be the last on the list. There are no outside places, and therefore there is no hope of any relief from the horrors of a hot day and a full coach.

The "drivers," whom it would be treason to call *coachmen*, change, with their teams, every fourteen or sixteen miles, are kind to their horses, and drive with "the reins in both hands," as they say in "Ould Ireland," "and the whip in the other." They are little,

M 5

round-shouldered rascals, sitting on the box
with their chins almost resting on their knees,
and arms extended to full length, clean their
own horses, and drive them entirely in snaffle-
bits, giving them great quantities of water,
three or four times during the stage : upon
occasion, the coach is driven bodily into ponds,
rivers, or lakes. In America, as on the
Continent, carriages are always passed on
the right hand. England is the only country
where the reverse is practised, and her children in the New World have adopted the
Continental practice in contradistinction, I
suppose, to the habits of the mother-country ; but,

> The laws of the road are a paradox quite,
> For when you are travelling along,
> If you keep to the *left* you'll be sure to be *right*,
> If you keep to the *right* you'll be *wrong*.

Nations differ as to the treatment of horses
on a journey; a Yankee will give them as
much water as they can drink to induce them

to " go ahead;" in England it is considered
to have a contrary effect ; the Italian vettu-
rino employs a head-dress of bells ; and Pat
is not without his own contrivance, a bundle
of hay, tied to the end of the pole, causing
a constant exertion to reach what is attained
only at the end of the journey. But the
ingenious inhabitant of the " Emerald Isle"
has many other such inventions. He will
open and slam-to the doors of a *post-chay*, to
flatter the animals into a belief that the
carriage has been lightened of its load.

Apropos to such Hibernian devices, I recollect being obliged to plead as an excuse to
a fair lady in Carlow for being late at her
dinner, the fact that the driver of our car,
having left us in the middle of the road,
in a downpour of rain, to light his " dudeen,"
a loose, half-starved horse, grazing in an
adjoining ditch, had taken a fancy to the
hay of which our traces and collars were
made, and eaten so much of it, that we

were detained till the harness was renewed. But the good old days when the post-chaises were thatched, one door nailed up, no steps to the other, and the ostler made his appearance with " a fork to raise the windies with, plase your honour," have vanished before the enlightened " tay-drink-ing" disciples of Father Matthew.

The country we passed through to North-ampton was but partially cleared, the tide of emigration having set to the west, the lands being there more fertile, requiring less labour and clearing, and to be had for less money.

We passed the Connecticut river by a covered wooden bridge, eleven hundred feet long, and arrived at Northampton, the *beau ideal* of a country village, with its white cottages and green jalousies ; magnificent and gigantic elms, single or in groups, part of the primeval forest, judiciously spared, added to its beauties. This is the fatherland of the Temperance system, which is carried to so disagreeable an extent that we were able to get only sour cider at the inns, and often not even that. A meeting in support of these doctrines was going on in the evening; an immense assemblage, chiefly of women, were edified by a man holding forth, till he worked himself into a perfect frenzy; we left him arguing strenuously that any person who sold spirituous liquors was a murderer in the sight of the Lord.

At our next halt, Pittsfield, we hired hacks, and visited a village of Shaking Quakers: they wear much the same kind of garb as their brethren in the Old World; but we could not see them shake, as they do that only when the spirit moves them. A communicative old gentleman of the persuasion told us the world had formed erroneous opinions of their women living in common— for, on the contrary, they separated man and wife.[1]

[1] This sect originated with a woman of the name of Anne Lee, of Manchester, who, having with her associates,

In this country of sectarians, the ceremony
of making a Baptist, and the ordeal they go
through, must be one of the least agreeable,

committed various offences against decorum, was glad to
take refuge in America. This woman, with her vulgar
and fanatical horde, under the name of *shakers* or *believers*,
established themselves at a town named Union, not far
from Cincinnati. Mr. Tell Harris, in a series of letters
published in London, thus describes these bedlamites: " The
bell for worship put an end to the discussion; the men, dis-
encumbering themselves of their coats and neckcloths,
formed into squares six deep; and, a pair of folding doors
being thrown back, discovered the women drawn up in the
like manner, each party having four on their right, who in
the sequel appeared to be the regulators of their motions:
two men then addressed the assembly on the manner in
which the Divine Being had been pleased to communicate
with some of his creatures, and that he still manifests himself to them by inspiration; quoting the example of David
and others, as proofs that dancing, singing, and clapping of
hands, are acceptable offerings of praise to him. A few
verses, the burden of which was 'dancing or agitation of the
frame, a sign of devotion,' were next sung, accompanied
with slight motions of the feet, increasing and exalting the
voice as they proceeded. The hymn being ended, a short
prayer was offered, that their hearts and lips might be
moved in praise; a general movement now of the feet took
place, accompanied with clapping of hands, twirling on
their heels, leaping, shouting, screaming, while the regulators on the flanks sung with some little variation, ' lo diddle!
ho diddle! lo diddle ho!' ceasing at intervals, to recover

particularly during the winter months : a hole is cut through the ice ; the candidate for baptism is lowered through, and up comes at once a Baptist and an icicle. Yet, notwithstanding what is before them, there are many who present themselves for immersion, or, as the knight's bard has it,

> To dive like wild-fowl for salvation,
> And fish to catch regeneration.

From Albany a railway took us to Saratoga, the Baden-Baden of the New World. The season was over, so we saw nothing of the amusements of the place. We met with a

from the violent exertions; some, however, unable to resist the violence of their feelings, continued to start suddenly, screaming and leaping in such a manner, that a stranger could not suppose them any other than unfortunates who had eluded the vigilance of their keepers. At the expiration of an hour, their worship ceased, perhaps from mere exhaustion; the men put on their coats, the women such of their caps and handkerchiefs as had been displaced in a twinkling, the folding doors separated them again, and each, by opposite doors, retired to their own apartments. I then left them, convinced and thankful that, to be a believer indeed, it is not necessary to be a Shaker."

gambler, who, finding that we were not be pigeoned, altered his tack, and turned out a most amusing dog. He was full of anecdotes of the South, and it actually ended in our determining to give up, for the present, our journey through Canada down the St. Lawrence, that we might proceed thither immediately after visiting Niagara.

We took the boat on the Erie canal from Schenectady to Utica, up the beautiful valley of the Mohawk—the canal running all the way parallel to the course of the river. This conveyance, always a bore, was made doubly so by the number of bridges we were obliged to pass under—so low that the man at the helm was obliged to sing out " Low Bridge," as we approached them, to the great terror of sundry fat gentlemen, who, not always looking ahead in time to get off the deck, were obliged to prostrate themselves on their backs; and the dismay in their faces evidently showed them to be calculating whether their large corpora-

tions would pass under unscathed. Narrow
as this kind of boat must of necessity be, it
was surprising how many beds they contrived
to make up: a long range of trays, three
deep, were let down from the cabin ceiling,
on which the beds were placed, connected
with cords somewhat in the manner of cottage
book-shelves; it was, therefore, desirable to
choose the highest berth, as the cords were
not over-strong; and, should the upper berth
be occupied by any one at all approaching to
Daniel Lambert's calibre, the chances were
that he would carry it away, and swamp the
unfortunate occupant of the primo piano.

The manner of steering these boats by
night is ingenious; two white goose-quills
are fastened upright on either extremity of
the deck, next the bow; a light from below is
reflected upon the feathers, which appear to
the man at the helm like two flames of fire.
We were not sorry to find ourselves at Utica,
and set off next day to see Trenton Falls,

which are fine in their way—a succession of
dark amber-coloured Falls, like the dark
waters of the Caernarvonshire rivers. From
Utica we had again to follow the Erie canal
as far as Syracuse; whence, skirting a long
lake, we descended the Oswego river, as far
as the town of that name, situated at its
outlet in Lake Ontario. Here we embarked
in a steamer on its dark blue waters, and by
sun-down had run the land out of sight. The
following morning we landed at Toronto, the
capital of Upper Canada, which looked dirty
and uninteresting.

From Toronto the Transit steamer crossed
daily to Fort George, at the mouth of the
Niagara; in her we took our passage, and
were duly unshipped at the fort, where a
" stage " waited to convey passengers to the
Falls. The drive along the banks of the
Niagara river to Queenston is most lovely.
On the left flows the sea-green Niagara, its
banks covered with black walnut, hiccory,

acacia, and butternut trees, and on our right
stretched away fertile fields of Indian corn,
and orchards crowded with apple and peach
trees, the latter in such quantities, that the
pigs are fed on the fruit. This beautiful
scenery continues to Queenston, half-way
from the town of Niagara to the Falls, where
we had to climb a hill, on the summit of which
is erected a well-executed column to Sir Isaac
Brock, who drove the Americans over the
river in 1812. The view from this monument is one of the finest I ever looked upon.
Beneath, the river, green as a vein of mala-
chite, flows through the above described rich
country, until it meets Ontario, which is
bounded in the far horizon by blue outlines
of hills some sixty miles distant.

Evidently the Falls commenced at this
point, breaking their way up to their present
site, seven miles further, where they have had
a check, and where, in all probability, they
will ever remain; for, so long as the river

was confined to a narrow space, they continually receded. At present, the mass of
water is broken into two Falls, checked for
ever by the extended width of the current.
Small fragments may wear away and break
off, as did a small piece of the Table Rock a
few years ago, and some such event was the
probable origin of the famous hoax in the
Buffalo paper, stating the cataract to have
entirely disappeared ; but, for ages to come,
the Falls of Niagara must bear the same
character, and be confined to their present
locale. A few inches they may recede, which
can only add to their sublimity.

One of the party, who was all anxiety and
excitement, had extended himself at full
length upon the top or rather roof of " the
stage"—outside places, as before stated, exist
not in the contrivances of the New World
which do duty for coaches—and had taken
up this position, fancying that he should get
first view of the Falls. Indeed, all one's

"auricular" nerves were on the stretch to catch the slightest murmurs of the mighty cataracts, and the veriest zephyr was enough to draw forth an ejaculation. We were now close to them, and, passing through an oak forest, the branches from which frequently swept the roof of the stage, suddenly our friend exclaimed — "Listen! — there they are! — don't you hear them?" As he uttered the last word, we heard a distinct murmur, a decided rippling noise, followed by an execration; and it was instantly apparent whence the noise had proceeded — a bough of a huge oak had hitched in the nether end of our friend's best Stulz "cut-away" coat, and had divided it completely up the back to the very shoulders—this of course caused a hearty laugh, in which he most good-humouredly joined. The torn habiliment was skewered together in the best manner that we could contrive; and soon afterwards we began to hear distinctly the roar of waters, and another half hour brought us to the Falls of Niagara.

No one can, either by description of pen or pencil, give the smallest idea of these Falls. It is as impossible as the endeavour of the artist to portray the Alps of Switzerland, the Jungfrau, or Mont Blanc. The best description I ever met with of Niagara, was a Yankee remark scribbled in Mr. Starkey's book of visitors who pass to Termination Rock,

"AN ALMIGHTY FALL OF WATER."

APPENDIX.

No. I.

From Mr. Gesner's Reports on New Brunswick.

The province contains about 16,5000,000 acres; of this 12,000,000 acres are capable of immediate cultivation, and 1,000,000 may be reclaimed in a more advanced state of agriculture. I have estimated that, including the great marshes of Westmoreland, only 440,000 acres are cleared.[1] By obtaining a credit of the government for fifty acres of land, any person, with a family, having a capital of £12 currency (£9 12s. sterling), can maintain such family until the first crop is produced; and, with sobriety and industry, in six years he can pay for the land with the interest on the first pur-

---

[1] From official returns, 3,634,280 acres have been granted, and 13,792,272 remain at the disposal of the Crown.

chase, and purchase fifty acres more on credit. The above may be performed in less time than six years; but I have taken this period as a medium estimate.

The lands along the southern coast of the province are in general much less fit for cultivation than those of the interior and northern shores. The settlers are also exposed to the dense fogs of the coast, but which seldom reach more than twenty miles from the seaboard. The soil, from being derived from granite and other hard rock, is more scanty along the southern coast; and it is frequently too strong to be extensively cultivated. There are, nevertheless, many small tracts of good upland, and some fine intervals along the rivers and smaller streams.

Twenty miles from the southern seaboard, the lands improve, and the whole northern side of the province may be said to be capable of being tilled to advantage. The quality of the soil, however, differs in different districts; and there are many extensive tracts of waste land of a superior quality. The several counties have been classed in regard to the lands they contain fit for immediate settlement, in the following order :—

St. John. There is but a very limited quantity of good ungranted land in this county. The lands eastward of Quaco, and those recently laid out between Quaco and Hammond river, are in general broken and stony, and the gravelly nature of the soil is seldom discovered until the land is cleared of its timber; there are but few intervales [1] in this county.

King's County. There is a large area of superior land for settlement southward of Sussex vale, and at the head of the mill stream.

Westmorland. In the county of Westmorland there still remain some fine ungranted tracts; they are chiefly situated at the heads of Pollet and Coverdale rivers, and Turtle Creek, and also at the sources of the Washademoak. The soil in general is a sandy loam, and it is easily worked. There are some intervales still ungranted.

Queen's. In Queen's county there are a number of tracts of excellent ungranted land. There is a large tract between the Nerepis Road and Gagetown, including the Victoria settlement; also, southward of the Nerepis Road, upon both sides of the Washademoak river, above Long's Creek, and between Salmon river and New Canaan settlement. Some of these soils are a deep red loam. Limestone was found to be abundant on both sides of the

---

[1] Alluvial flats adjacent to the rivers, which are annually overflowed, and yield abundant hay-crops.

St. John: it will be seen at the farm of Mr. Merritt, and at the south entrance of the Washademoak.

Charlotte. The best ungranted lands in this county were seen in the direction of the Magaguadavie river: and there are intervales along the principal streams. The northern part of this county abounds in granite rocks. The lands in the Tryon settlement are in general rocky, and a part of the soil is meagre.

Sunbury. Almost all the ungranted land in this county is of a good quality, and probably not more than one half of its surface is disposed of. There are some good intervales.

York. The best ungranted lands in this county are situated on the south-east side of the Nashwaak, and near the main south-west Miramichi and Taxas river.

Carleton. Almost all the lands in this county are of a superior quality. Between the St. John and the main south-west Miramichi, there is an immense tract of fertile soil, with belts of intervale along the streams. Very extensive settlements might be opened in this quarter. Farther westward there is a mountainous ridge; even here there are some superior lands, and the scenery is truly Alpine. The Tobique river passes through a fine

country for agriculture, where gypsum and limestone are abundant. The river is skirted with
excellent intervales. These lands are not granted,
and offer every advantage for settlement. Near
the banks of the St. John, the Grand Falls, and at
Grand River, the land is good, and limestone is
plentifully scattered over the county.

Kent. There are some good soils in this county ;
many of them are, however, light and sandy.

Northumberland. The good land in this county
is too extensive to require any particular description, and there is much intervale along the streams.

Gloucester. The above remark will apply to the
north-eastern part of Gloucester. There are,
nevertheless, some low and swampy grounds in
this quarter.

Restigouche. The lands near the mouth of the
Restigouche are mountainous and broken. Southward of Dalhousie and Campbelltown there is a
large tract of superior land ; upon a part of this
tract the Colebrooke settlement is situated. There
are good lands upon the upper part of the river.
The interior of Gloucester and Restigouche counties
have not been explored.

No. II.

RETURN showing the Average Retail Price of Provisions and Clothing in the Colony of New Brunswick, in the quarter endeḍ 31st Dec., 1845.

ARTICLES.	Quantity.	Average Prices in Sterling.		
		£	s.	d.
Salt beef	per lb.	0	0	3½
Fresh ditto	,,	0	0	3
Mutton	,,	0	0	3
Lamb	,,	0	0	3
Veal	,,	0	0	3
Fresh pork	,,	0	0	2½
Salt ditto	,,	0	0	3½
Fowls	per pair	0	1	3
Bacon	per lb.	0	0	4
Salt butter	,,	0	0	9
Fresh ditto	,,	0	0	10
Fresh milk	per quart	0	0	3
Cheese	per lb.	0	0	5
Eggs	per dozen	0	0	9
Potatoes	per bushel	0	3	0
Bread, best wheaten . . .	4lb. loaf	0	0	9
Ditto, seconds	6lb. loaf	0	0	10
Best wheat flour	barrel 196 lbs.	1	15	0
Second quality ditto . . .	,,	1	10	0
Oatmeal	per cwt.	0	9	0
Coals	per chaldron	1	2	6
Candles	per lb.	0	0	9
Firewood, cord of 128 cubic ft.	. . . . .	1	0	0
Common soap	per lb.	0	0	4½
Tea	,,	0	2	0
Coffee (green)	,,	0	0	10
Rice	,,	0	0	3
Sugar, brown	,,	0	0	5
Ditto, loaf	,,	0	0	6½
Salt	per bushel	0	1	4
Pepper	per lb.	0	0	10
Salt fish, dry, the cheapest .	per quintal	0	10	0
Ditto, green	the barrel	0	16	3
Beer	per gallon	0	1	6
Porter, London	per bottle	0	0	10
Men's stout shoes	per pair	0	6	3
Women's ditto	,,	0	5	0
Snow over-shoes	,,	0	10	0
Men's shirts, cotton . . .	each	0	3	4
Flannel	per yard	0	1	6
Cloth for coats	,,	0	7	6
Cotton for gowns	,,	0	0	7
Fustian	,,	0	1	3
Velveteen	,,	0	2	3

M. H. PERLEY, Government Emigration Agent.

No. III.

RETURN showing the Average Wages of Mechanics and others in the Colony of New Brunswick, for the 3 Months ended 31st Dec., 1845.

Trade or Calling.	Average Wages per Diem without Board and Lodging, in Sterling.	Average Wages per Diem with Board and Lodging, in Sterling.	Average Wages per Annum with Board and Lodging, in Sterling.	Highest & Lowest Rates per Diem without Board or Lodging, (in Sterling.)	
				Highest.	Lowest.
Bread and biscuit	s. d. s. d.	s. d. s. d.	£ s. d.		
bakers . . .	. . .	. . .	20 0 0		
Butchers . . .	4 6	2 6	32 0 0		
Brickmakers . .	3 0 to 5 0	2 0 to 3 6			
Bricklayers . .	5 0 to 6 6	3 0 to 5 0			
Blacksmiths . .	5 0	3 0	30 0 0		
Curriers . . .	5 0	3 0	33 0 0		
Carpenters and					
joiners . . .	5 6	3 6	35 0 0		
Cabinetmakers .	5 6	3 9	35 0 0		
Coopers . . .	4 9	3 0	30 0 0		
Carters	4 6	3 0	24 0 0		
Cooks (women) .	. . .	. . .	10 0 0		
Combmakers . {	No employ- ment.				
Dairywomen . .	. . .	. . .	7 10 0		
Dressmakers and					
milliners . . .	2 3	1 3	10 0 0		
Farm labourers .	3 0	1 3	18 0 0		
Gardeners . . .	4 6	3 0	25 0 0		
Grooms	. . .	. . .	18 0 0		
Millwrights . .	6 0	4 0	40 0 0		
Millers	5 6	4 0	32 0 0		
Painters . . .	5 6	3 6			
Plasterers . . .	5 6	4 0			
Plumbers and {	Very little				
glaziers . . {	employment.				
Quarrymen . .	3 0	1 3	18 0 0		
Ropemakers . .	. . .	. . .	35 0 0		
Sailmakers . .	. . .	5 6	32 10 0		
Sawyers . . .	4 0 to 6 0	2 6 to 4 6	32 10 0		
Shepherds . {	No employ- ment.				
Shipwrights and					
boatbuilders .	3 9 to 5 0	2 0 to 4 0	30 0 0		
Shoemakers . .	3 6 to 4 0	2 6 to 3 0	26 0 0		
Slaters & shinglers	5 0	3 6			
Stonemasons . .	4 0 to 5 6	3 0 to 4 0	32 10 0		
Tailors	. . .	. . .	30 0 0		
Tanners . . .	. . .	. . .	35 0 0		
Wheelwrights .	. . .	. . .	35 0 0		
Whitesmiths . .	4 6	3 0	28 0 0		

M. H. PERLEY—G. E. A.

No. IV.

ABSTRACT RETURN of IMMIGRATION to NEW BRUNSWICK, during the Year ending 31st December, 1845.

Quarters.	No. of Vessels Arrived.	No. of deaths on board or in Quarantine.	No. of births on board or in Quarantine.	Adults Male.	Adults Female.	Children between 14 years and 1 year. Male.	Children between 14 years and 1 year. Female.	Children under 1 year. Male.	Children under 1 year. Female.	Totals Male.	Totals Female.	No. of Souls.
Quarter ending 31st March .	nil	—	—	—	—	—	—	—	—	—	—	—
Quarter ending 31st June . .	43	9	3	2048	2171	327	401	84	83	2459	2655	5114
Quarter ending 30th Sept . .	25	9	—	322	391	103	102	20	18	445	511	956
Quarter ending 31st Dec. . .	2	—	—	14	33	6	8	1	1	21	42	63
Totals . .	70	9	3	2384	2595	436	511	105	102	2925	3208	6133

Recapitulation

	Male.	Female.
Adults . . . . From 14 to 1 yr	2384	2595
	436	511
Under 1 year	105	102
Totals .	2925	3208
In all, 6,133 souls.		

Government Emigration Office, St. John, New Brunswick.

31st December, 1845.

M. H. PERLEY.

No V

RETURN, showing the prices of Agricultural Produce, Farming Stock, and implements of Husbandry in the colony of New Brunswick, on the 31st December, 1845.

Articles.	Quantity.	Sterling Dollars at 4s. 2d. each.			Remarks.
		£	s.	d.	
Wheat . . .	per bushel	0	5	9	
Barley . . .	do.	0	3	9	Large quantities of each imported from abroad.
Rye	do.	0	3	9	
Oats . . .	do.	0	2	6	
Maize . . .	do.	0	5	6	
Buckwheat . .	do.	0	3	9	
Beans . . .	do.	0	0	0	Not cultivated for sale.
Peas	do.	0	6	3	
Potatoes . .	do.	0	3	0	
Hay	per ton	3	0	0	Potatoes are excessively bad and dear, owing to the failure of the crop.
Good Cart Horse	about	15	0	0	
Useful riding ditto	,,	20	0	0	
Yoke of Oxen .	,,	18	0	0	
Sheep, per score	,,	9	0	0	
Good Milch Cow	,,	5	0	0	
Breeding Sow .	,,	1	15	0	
Pigs, each . .	,,	0	4	6	
A cart of the description used by farmers	about	7	10	0	
A Waggon ditto	,,	10	0	0	
A Plough . .	,,	2	10	6	
Harrow . . .	,,	1	10	0	
Country Plough	,,	2	0	0	
Sledge for winter	,,	3	10	0	

Government Emigration Office, St. John, New Brunswick,

M. H. PERLEY.

31st December, 1845.

No. VI.

REFLEXIONS ON THE PRESENT STATE OF NEW
BRUNSWICK IN REFERENCE TO A PROPOSED LINE
OF RAILWAY.

Government Emigration Office,
St. John, N. B., Nov. 10, 1845.

Sir,

Since forwarding my last quarterly return, I
have received various documents addressed to me
officially, by persons in England, relative to the
formation of a railway from Halifax to Quebec,
through this province, and proposing the colo-
nization and settlement of the line of country
traversed, in connection therewith. As the pro-
posal expressly refers to immigration on a large
scale, I have felt it my duty to bring the subject
under His Excellency's consideration, and at the
same time respectfully to offer some remarks upon
the matter as connected with the business of this
office.

It may be considered as a settled principle in
England, that, whether for facilitating commerce,
or improving land, railways are the best instru-
ments that can be used. If such be the case in

England, abounding as it does in wealth, in a high
state of cultivation, with the best and most numerous means of inter-communication, and teeming
with population, what would be the effect of railways in a young country like New Brunswick, yet
poor and struggling into existence, with but few
and imperfect roads, and a population which barely
reaches one soul to every hundred acres of its
extent?

If the difficulties attendant upon the settlement
of a new country be taken into consideration, there
can be no doubt that much has been effected in
New Brunswick within the brief period which has
elapsed since its first settlement by British subjects. Yet all that has been done is comparatively
trifling, when considered with reference to the
extent of country yet ungranted and uncultivated,
and the abundant resources it possesses. As a
field for the pursuits of agriculture, the prosecution
of commercial enterprise, and the formation of
flourishing settlements, this colony offers powerful
inducements. It is blessed with a rich and pro-
ductive soil; it abounds with trees of the greatest
utility and value, and is watered by innumerable
rivers and streams. It rejoices in skies that are
bright and cheerful, and a climate salubrious in the
extreme, congenial to the growth, not only of the

N 5

necessaries, but many of the luxuries of life. Above all, it has the happiness to enjoy institutions and forms of government, modelled upon their proto-types in the mother-country, which secure British laws, and British freedom to all its inhabitants.

With these numerous advantages, it may be asked, why New Brunswick has not made greater strides in the progress of improvement, and why its population is yet so scanty. The reply is, that the want of roads and efficient means of communi-cation keep the great body of the country yet in a state of unbroken wilderness, isolates it from the neighbouring colony of Canada, deprives it of com-mercial avenues, and renders the progress of settle-ment and improvement so very slow, in comparison with what might reasonably be expected from the bounties which nature has lavished upon it.

In considering this subject, it is important to state the extent of wilderness in New Brunswick and the progress of its population, as to which, I beg to submit the following statistics.

The area of this province is estimated in round numbers at seventeen millions of acres—of these five millions are said to be granted—two millions are deducted for water and waste, and the remaining ten millions, all fit for settlement and cultivation, are yet in a state of wilderness, ungranted, and at the disposal of the government. The ungranted lands are thus distributed :—

In Restigouche and Gloucester counties .	1,828,000	acres.
„ Northumberland . . .	2,216,000	„
„ Kent	552,400	„
„ Westmorland	532,000	„
„ Saint John	126,000	„
„ Charlotte	480,000	„
„ King's	244,000	„
„ Queen's	470,000	„
„ Sunbury	413,000	„
„ York	1,280,000	„
„ Carleton	2,080,000	„
Total . . .	10,221,000	acres.

With regard to population, the increase stands thus :—

In 1783 (province established,)	12,000	souls.
„ 1803	27,000	„
„ 1824	74,176	„
„ 1834 . . .	119,457	„
„ 1840 . . .	156,162	„

Prior to the year 1818, partial emigration from the United Kingdom had occasionally taken place to this colony; but after that period it began to flow in a regular and steady stream. From 1824 to 1834, the emigrants to New Brunswick amounted to 48,000; yet the increase of population between those periods was only 45,000. From 1834 to

1840, the increase of population was 36,000—a number far short of the immigrants who arrived in the province during the same period. It is clear, therefore, that New Brunswick is not greatly indebted to immigration for the increase of its population during the last twenty years, which may be principally attributed to the natural multiplication of its inhabitants.

The immigration of the present season has somewhat exceeded six thousand souls—about one half of whom have departed for the United States, attracted by the greater demand for labour there, and by the cheapness and rapidity of travelling, by steamers and railways, which enable immigrants to reach the western country, where fertile lands can be procured on easy terms, and where every facility exists for transmitting farming produce to the Atlantic sea-ports and a ready market. It cannot but be matter of regret, that so many of Her Majesty's subjects, who cross the Atlantic and arrive annually in this colony, cannot be settled on vacant crown lands, but should pass through this fine province, and become, more through necessity than choice, the subjects of a foreign government.

I have repeatedly had the honour to state, in my reports on immigration, that the remedy for this

untoward state of things would be the commencement of some great public or private work in New
Brunswick, tending to open up the interior of the
country—and none would seem to be better adapted
for the desired end than the establishment of the
proposed line of railway through the heart of the
province.

It will not escape His Excellency's observation,
that, of the ungranted lands in the colony, there is
not more than one-tenth west of the river St. John,
and that the remaining nine-tenths are to the eastward of that river. The formation of a line of
railway through this vast tract of wilderness would
afford abundant employment for a long period to an
immense number of emigrant labourers, who would
thus become acquainted with the work of the
country, and be trained up to the necessary dexterity and skill essential to the success of settlers
in the forest. By means of cross roads and
branches, assisted by the infinity of lakes, rivers,
and streams, every part of the province would be
rendered readily accessible, and the farmer in the
remotest district would possess the means of reaching market with ease and certainty. No objection
would exist, as at present, against taking up land
in the interior of the country, where the soil is
excellent, on account of its solitude, the difficulty

of reaching it, or the almost impossibility of bringing its products to a market.

The numberless advantages which would be afforded by a railway through New Brunswick, connecting it with the neighbouring colonies of Canada and Nova Scotia, would for many years render it capable of absorbing annually thousands and tens of thousands of immigrants from the United Kingdom, who would find a happy home in a British colony, where they could maintain their allegiance to their sovereign, and by prudence and industry attain to comfort and independence as freeholders and lords of the soil. Every accession of population, whether composed of indigent or wealthy individuals, provided it consists of able-bodied men, would be highly desirable in a country where land is abundant and inhabitants comparatively few.

It does not fall within the line of my duty to animadvert upon the effects which the proposed line of railway would have upon the mercantile interests of New Brunswick, by facilitating commercial intercourse, and opening up new sources of trade, by developing the mineral wealth and great natural resources of the country. But I may, however, be permitted, in conclusion, to observe, that a railway to unite the colonies of Canada, New Brunswick,

and Nova Scotia, into one common bond of union,
by drawing together their remotest extremities,
uniting their energies, and consolidating their
strength, cannot be viewed otherwise than as a
great national object. The slow progress of settlement and tardy increase of population would thereby
be accelerated "with railroad speed," and greater
progress in those respects would be made in ten
years under the influence of railways, than under
the present order of things will probably take place
during the next century. The advantages offered
to these colonies by railway communication are so
varied, so numerous, and so overwhelming, as
scarcely to be within the grasp of the most compre-
hensive mind, but would inevitably lead to results
alike glorious to British North America, and the
great empire of which it forms a favoured portion.

I have the honour to be,

M. H. PERLEY,

Government Emigration Agent.

Alfred Reade, Esq.,
Private Secretary, &c., Fredericton.

No. VII.

NOTES ON THE TREES OF NEW BRUNSWICK.

Gray Oak—*Quercus Borealis,* or *Quercus Ambigua.*

Red Oak—*Quercus Rubra.*— Neither of much value from their small size.

Butternut—*Juglans Cathartica,* attains a large size and bears abundance of large nuts of good flavour ; wood much used at present by cabinet-makers.

White Maple—*Acer Eriocarpum.*—Very pretty white wood, not unlike sycamore. When spotted, it is called Bird's-eye Maple.

Red-flowering Maple—*Acer Rubrum.*

Sugar Maple—*Acer Saccharinum.*—Maple sugar is made from this tree.

Moose Wood—*Acer Striatum.*—The name of moose-wood was given to this species of maple by the first settlers, from observing that the moose, an animal now becoming scarce in this region, subsisted during the latter part of the winter and beginning of spring on its young twigs. The moose-wood bears a very large flower, which when beginning to unfold is rose-coloured, but afterwards pure white. This tree is found most vigorous in mixed forests, when the woods are composed of the sugar maple, the beech, white birch, yellow birch, and hemlock spruce. In these forests it constitutes a great part of the under growth.

Mountain Maple—*Acer Montanum*, called low maple in New Brunswick.

Dog Wood—*Cornus Florida.*—Among the eight species of dog-wood which have been observed in North America, this species alone is entitled by its size to be classed with the forest trees. It is most interesting from the beauty of its flowers.

Canoe Birch—*Betula Papyracea.*—The canoe birch attains its largest size, which is about seventy feet in height and three feet in diameter, on the declivity of hills and in the bottom of fertile valleys ; its branches are slender, flexible, and covered with a shining brown bark, dotted with white. The heart or perfect wood of this tree, when first laid open, is of a reddish hue, and the sap is perfectly white. The wood has a fine glossy grain, and considerable strength. Tables and other furniture are frequently made of it, and stained in imitation of mahogany. On trees not exceeding eight inches in diameter, the bark is of a brilliant white, and is almost indestructible by time.

The bark of the birch is applied to a great variety

of uses. It forms the wigwam of the Indian, and many, if not all, his utensils in the forest. The settlers place large sheets of it immediately beneath the shingles of the roof, to form a more impenetrable cover for their houses. Baskets, boxes, and portfolios are made of it : the latter are frequently embroidered with silk or moose hair, dyed in a great variety of most brilliant colours.

But of the many uses to which it is applied, none is more important than the construction of canoes, and for this purpose it cannot be replaced by the bark of any other tree. To procure a proper piece for a canoe, the largest and smoothest trunk is selected. When the tree is felled, a longitudinal incision is made along the tree for twenty or twenty-five feet ; two circular incisions are made at each end ; the bark is loosened a little with the knife or a wedge, and almost immediately springs from the tree.

To form the canoe, the seams are stitched with the fibrous roots of the white spruce about the size of a quill, which are deprived of the bark, split, and suppled in water. The seams are coated with the gum of the spruce or balsam fir.

White Birch—*Betula Populifolia.*—The trunk of this species is clothed in a bark of as pure a white as that of the canoe birch, but its epidermis, when separated from the cellular integument, is incapable of being divided into thin sheets, which constitutes an essential difference.

Yellow Birch—*Betula Lutea.*—Chiefly used for fuel.

Black Birch — *Betula Lenta*, or *Betula Nigra.*— This tree forms the birch timber, of which large quantities are annually exported : it is also much used in ship-building.

Common Alder—*Alnus Serrulata.*

Wild Cherry-tree—*Cerasus Virginiana.*

Red Cherry-tree—*Cerasus Borealis.*—Both these bear abundance of fruit, of a pleasant flavour but slightly acrid.   The fruit makes capital *cherry bounce.*

Balm of Gilead, or Balsam Poplar—*Populus Balsamifera.*

American Aspen, or Common Poplar—*Populus Tremuloides.*

White Beech—*Fagus Sylvestris.*—Red Beech— *Fagus Ferruginea.*—Very common ; the white beech is valuable for ship-building, particularly for floor timber and bottom planks.

Hornbeam—*Carpinus Virginiana.*—Not very common ; wood very hard and heavy.   Hornbeam is valuable for every purpose to which its small size permits it to be applied.

Iron Wood—*Carpinus Ostrya.*

White Ash—*Fraxinus Americana.*

Black Ash—*Fraxinus Sambucifolia.*—The black ash is comparatively of little value to the white ash, of which great use is made in North America for almost every purpose. Coachmakers use it for shafts, frames of carriages, bodies, sleighs, and sleds. It is useful for chairs, water-pails, butter-boxes, sieves, spinning-wheels, hay-rakes, and numberless other purposes.

White Elm—*Ulmus Americana.*

Red Elm—*Ulmus Rubra.*

Bass Wood, or American Lime—*Tilia Americana.*

Red Pine—*Pinus Rubra;* in Canada *Pin Rouge,* and by the settlers Norway Pine.—Large quantities exported.

Gray Pine—*Pinus Rupestris.*—Not common; of little value.

White Pine—*Pinus Strobus.*—This is the great timber pine of commerce, generally called by timbermen, "the pumpkin pine," from its softness and whiteness. The largest trees grow in the bottoms of soft, friable, and fertile valleys, on the banks of rivers composed of deep cool, black sand, and in swamps filled with the white cedar, and covered with a thick and constantly humid carpet of *spagnum.* This ancient and majestic inhabitant of the North American forests is still the loftiest and most valuable of their productions, and its summit is seen at an immense distance aspiring towards heaven, far above the heads of the surrounding trees.

American Silver Fir, or Balm of Gilead Fir—*Abies Balsamifera.*—From this tree the well-known Canadian Balsam is obtained. This substance is naturally deposited in vesicles on the trunk and limbs, and is collected by bursting these tumours and receiving their contents in a bottle.

White Cedar—*Cupressis Thyoides.*—The foliage is evergreen : the wood is light, soft, fine-grained, and easily wrought. When perfectly seasoned, and exposed for some time to the light, it is of a rosy hue ; it has a strong aromatic odour, which it preserves as long as it is guarded from humidity. The perfect wood resists the succession of dryness and moisture longer than that of any other species, and for this quality it is much valued. It is now much used for fishing-boats, and all the boats used by the whalers are built of it.

American Larch—*Laryx Americana.*—The Indian name is Hackmatack. The early Dutch settlers named it *Tamarack*—the French Canadians call it *Epinette Rouge.* In the northern parts of New Brunswick, where it is extensively used in

ship-building, it is called Juniper. The wood of
the American Larch is superior to any species of
pine or spruce, and unites all the properties which
distinguish the European species, being exceedingly
strong and singularly durable. Turpentine is never
extracted from it in America, as is done from the
native species in Europe. The American Larch is
a magnificent tree, with a straight, slender trunk,
eighty or one hundred feet in length and two or
three feet in diameter. Its numerous branches,
except near the summit, are horizontal or declining.
The bark is smooth and polished on the trunk and
longer limbs, and rugged on the smaller branches.

Black (double) Spruce—*Abies Nigra.*—In Canada, this spruce is called *Epinette Noire*, and
Epinette à la bière. The knees of vessels are generally formed of black spruce, and immense quantities are annually sawn in New Brunswick into
deals (or planks three inches thick) for exportation.
From the young branches is made the salutary
drink known as " spruce beer." The twigs are
boiled in water, a certain quantity of molasses or
maple sugar is added, with a little yest, and the
mixture is left to ferment. The " essence of spruce"
is obtained by evaporating to the consistence of an
extract. Spruce beer is an effectual preventive of
scurvy. The fishermen of Newfoundland and the

Gulf of St. Lawrence drink large quantities of the spruce beer, mixed with rum, which drink they call " callibogus." It is considered an admirable corrective of their diet of very fat pork, (clear sheer) and keeps the men in good health. If the beer is made with white sugar and the rum be old, the drink is excellent.

White (single) Spruce—*Abies Alba.*—In Canada *Epinette blanche.*—Much inferior to the foregoing.

Hemlock Spruce—*Abies Canadensis.*—The hemlock spruce is always larger and taller than the black spruce. It attains the height of seventy or eighty feet, with a circumference of six to nine feet, and uniform for two-thirds of its length. Moist grounds appear not to be in general the most favourable to its growth. In size it falls far short of the white pine, or *pinus strobus*, which is the giant of American forests. Hemlock bark is extensively used for tanning in New Brunswick ; no other bark is used for that purpose.

American Arbor Vitæ, or White Cedar—*Thuya Occidentalis.*—This is the most multiplied of the resinous trees, after the black and hemlock spruces. A cool soil is indispensable to its growth. It is seldom seen on the uplands among the beeches and birches, but is found on the rocky edges of the innumerable rivulets and small lakes scattered over this country. It frequently occupies in great part, or exclusively, swamps from fifty to one hundred acres in extent, some of which are accessible only in the winter when frozen.

The branches of the white cedar will keep off moths when placed amongst clothes or furs. Boxes of red cedar (cedar of Lebanon) will do the same, as also sandalwood. It is the powerful odour which has the effect upon the moths, and which they cannot bear. A more curious fact is that rats will not gnaw the wood of the hemlock-spruce, and therefore in New Brunswick it is used for corn-bins, ceiling cook-cellars, &c. The wood is said to be very bitter and poisonous : at all events, rats will not touch it—a hemlock plank often stops their depredations.

There is no native Willow in New Brunswick which can rank as a tree ; and I have some doubts whether the Alder should be classed as such.

The foregoing list comprises all the forest trees yet known or noticed in New Brunswick. Future research may discover others, but they cannot exist in any quantity or to any extent.

No. VIII.

ON THE FOREST TREES OF NEW BRUNSWICK.

SUBSTANCE OF A LECTURE DELIVERED BY M. H. PERLEY, ESQ., AT THE MECHANICS' INSTITUTE.

In introducing the subject, the lecturer said that, in order to elucidate it clearly, it would be necessary to take a brief glance at the geographical position of New Brunswick, and notice some of its principal features. A large map of the province was exhibited, and the lecturer said, that the area of the province, in round numbers, was seventeen millions of acres : that of these seventeen millions, five millions were granted, and two millions were deducted for water and waste, leaving ten millions ungranted and all fit for settlement at the disposal of the Crown. Of the five millions granted, only 500,000 acres were officially reported as being cleared and cultivated ; and, deducting this quantity, with a liberal allowance for water and waste, it would be seen that New Brunswick contained no less than fourteen millions of acres, covered with a dense forest.

The southern part of the province (St. Andrew's) was stated as being in lat. 45° north, and Dalhousie, the northern extreme, in lat. 48°. The trees which covered the country were described as those which

flourish in greatest perfection between the parallels of 43° and 46° north, and might be divided
into two great classes. The first class comprises
the resinous trees, such as the pines and spruces,
which cover the low grounds and bottoms of the
valleys ; these are called " Soft wood lands." The
second class consists of the deciduous or leafy trees,
such as the maple, birch, and beech ; these grow
on level ground or gentle declivities, and form what
are called " Hard wood lands."

Between the 43rd and 46th parallels, these two
great classes are found in nearly equal proportions ;
but, proceeding from the 46th degree northward,
the leafy trees become more rare, and the resinous
trees more abundant. Below the 43rd degree, on
the other hand, proceeding to the south, the resinous trees are found less common, and the others
soon lose their predominance in the forest, by becoming mingled with the numerous species of oaks
and walnuts.

The lecturer stated, that in North America, beyond the parallel of 48°, all trees become dwarfish
and but few varieties are found ; that beyond 49°,
only dwarfish shrubs exist up to 50° north, beyond
which there are only mosses and barrens, across
that extensive tract of country stretching from
Canada to the Arctic Ocean.

It was clear from the lecturer's statements, that this province, situated between the parallels of 45° and 48°, occupies a favourable position on the continent of North America for furnishing a variety of large and valuable forest trees. Of these, the lecturer said he had prepared a list, which he now for the first time submitted to the public—he was not aware that any similar list had been heretofore prepared, and he offered this as the result of the information he had derived from the works of the best naturalists, and of his own observations during some years among the forests, in different parts of the province. It was not offered as a perfect and complete list ; but he trusted that, so far as it went, it would be found correct.

The lecturer then entered into a detailed description of several species mentioned in the list, and exhibited some very fine specimens of native wood, particularly butternut, of good size and excellent quality, from the valley of the St. John, and larch and poplar of fine quality and large size, from Miramichi.

Subjoined is a correct copy of the list of forest trees exhibited at the lecture :—

Oak—Two species.

| Gray Oak | . | . | . | *Quercus Borealis.* |
| Red Oak | . | . | . | *Quercus Rubra.* |

Walnut—One species.

Butternut   .   .   .   *Juglans Cathartica.*

Maple—Five species.

White Maple   .   .   .   *Acer Eriocarpum.*
Red-flowering Maple   .   *Acer Rubrum.*
Sugar (Rock) Maple   .   *Acer Saccharinum.*
Moose Wood   .   .   .   *Acer Striatum.*
Mountain (Low) Maple   .   *Acer Montanum.*

Cornus—One species.

Dog Wood   .   .   .   *Cornus Florida.*

Birch—Four species.

Canoe Birch   .   .   .   *Betula Papyracea.*
White Birch   .   .   .   *Betula Populifolia.*
Yellow Birch   .   .   .   *Betula lutea.*
Black Birch   .   .   .   *Betula lenta.*

Alder—One species.

Common Alder   .   .   *Alnus Serrulata.*

Cherry—Two species.

Wild Cherry Tree   .   .   *Cerasus Virginiana.*
Red Cherry Tree   .   .   *Cerasus Borealis.*

Poplar—Two species.

Balsam Poplar (Balm of Gilead) *Populus Balsamifera.*
American Aspen   .   .   *Populus Tremuloides.*

Beech—Two species.

White Beech   .   .   .   *Fagus Sylvestris.*
Red Beech   .   .   .   *Fagus Ferruginea.*

Carpinus—Two species.

American Hornbeam   .   *Carpinus Americana.*
Iron Wood   .   .   .   *Carpinus Ostrya.*

Ash—Two species.

White Ash   .   .   . *Fraxinus Americana.*

Black Ash   .   .   . *Fraxinus Sambucifolia.*

Willow—Three species.

Black Willow   .   . *Salix nigra.*

Champlain Willow   .   . *Salix lagustrina.*

Shining Willow   .   . *Salix lucida.*

Elm—Two species.

White Elm   .   .   . *Ulmus Americana.*

Red Elm   .   .   . *Ulmus Rubra.*

American Lime—One species.

Bass Wood   .   .   . *Tilia Americana.*

Pine—Three species.

Red (Norway) Pine   .   . *Pinus Rubra.*

Gray Pine   .   .   . *Pinus Rupestris.*

White Pine   .   .   . *Pinus Strobus.*

Spruce—Four species.

Black, or Double Spruce   *Abies Nigra.*

White, or Single Spruce   . *Abies Alba.*

Hemlock Spruce   .   . *Abies Canadensis.*

American Silver Fir   . *Abies Balsamifera.*

Cypress—One species.

White Cedar   .   .   . *Cupressis Thyoides.*

Larch—One species.

American Larch (Hackmatack)*Larix Americana.*

Juniper—One species.

Arbor Vitæ (Red Cedar)   . *Thuya Occidentalis.*

END OF VOL. I.

Frederick Shoberl, Junior, Printer to His Royal Highness Prince Albert,
51, Rupert Street, Haymarket, London.

For EU product safety concerns, contact us at Calle de José Abascal, 56–1°,
28003 Madrid, Spain or eugpsr@cambridge.org.

www.ingramcontent.com/pod-product-compliance
Ingram Content Group UK Ltd.
Pitfield, Milton Keynes, MK11 3LW, UK
UKHW040617240426
470322UK00010B/173